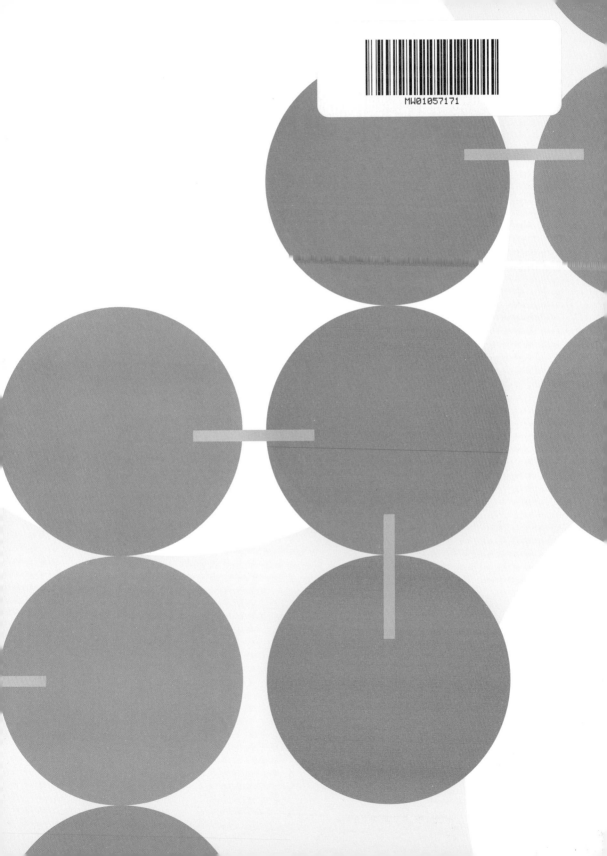

LUNCH
WELL

LUNCH
WELL

85 RECIPES TO BRING A **SPARK** TO THE MIDDAY MEAL

FERN GREEN

Photography by Kirstie Young

Hardie Grant
NORTH AMERICA

CONTENTS

INTRODUCTION

If you are looking for a modern recipe book to inspire you to create healthy weekday lunches from home, then look no further. Lunch has arrived. It's still as casual as breakfast, but it's more than just a sandwich.

Unlock the full potential of your workday with a better lunch. This cookbook is your passport to a world of delectable lunches crafted for the home office. From mouthwatering one-pan wonders to energizing salads and power bowls. There are over 80 recipes that will not only satisfy your palate, but will help you transform your mood.

Lunchtime can be used to create something that not only replenishes the body but also refreshes the mind. It can be casual like breakfast but it also needs to provoke a different interest to get you through the afternoon with vigor. Getting to midday after a full morning's work should be seen as time well spent and deserving of a break. It's time to introduce a nutritious ritual, where you can feel inspired and enthusiastic about creating and eating a tasty homemade lunch.

As your pantry is your toolkit and is as important as your fresh ingredients, this book will show you how to create recipes with only a few ingredients in your refrigerator and pantry. Alternatively, try turning one vegetable into three lunches—a modern take on batch cooking that leaves you with more time to concentrate on making satisfying flavors and textures.

THE IMPORTANCE OF LUNCH

Lunch plays a crucial role in our overall health and productivity throughout the day. See it as a time to pack in those nutrients. Perhaps you've skipped breakfast, or you are fasting, and this is your first meal of the day. Make sure it's a good one.

Energy boost → Lunch replenishes glucose levels and provides energy needed to sustain concentration and performance in the afternoon.

Nutrient intake → Lunch can contribute to the target of eating thirty different vegetables a week, which may improve gut health.

Metabolism regulation → Regular eating patterns help keep your metabolism steady and prevent your body going into starvation mode, which can lead to overeating.

Mental break → Taking time out for lunch provides a mental break, which reduces stress and improves focus and productivity for the rest of the day.

Weight management → Eating lunch can prevent overeating in the evening by curbing hunger and reducing the likelihood of snacking on unhealthy foods.

Alfresco → In the warmer months, and even the cold ones, it's good to get outside, breathe in the air, and change your focus. Call it "lunch meditation" if that helps.

MAKING THE MOST OF YOUR LUNCH BREAK

Spending the morning looking at a computer screen in the office or having back-to-back meetings at home online can make it hard for our brains to switch off from work mode into lunch mode, so you may need to make a few small changes to your habits.

Set a regular time → Try to schedule your lunch break at the same time each day to establish a routine that your brain and body can anticipate.

Physically step away from your desk → Go to a different room, preferably the kitchen or outside.

Try a physical activity → Whether it's taking a walk, chopping and preparing a salad, or engaging in a few minutes of deep breathing.

Avoid your phone or any screen → Try not to look at your phone, computer, or tablet for the allotted time you have given yourself.

Eat mindfully → Focus on the food, savor the flavors, and enjoy the act of eating. Mindful eating can enhance the pleasure of your meal and improve digestion.

Note:
You will find a lot of recipes in this book have methods where you use your hands to tear some leaves, pull off the ends of vegetables, grate a beet, and smash a cucumber. Feeling your food and promoting touch can create a mindful experience.

STRATEGIES FOR THE MIND & BODY

For the mind → Reduces your stress, improves your focus and concentration, enhances your creativity, and boosts your mood.
For the body → Increases nutrient intake, improves energy levels, metabolism support, improves digestion, helps with weight management and physical activity.

TOP FOOD HACKS WHILE MAKING COFFEE

If you start thinking about lunch when you boil the kettle, why not get ahead and start preparing your lunch? These are by no means necessary, just see them more as handy "get ahead" tricks for when your day is short on time. You can see them as useful "working from home" habits.

Seven-minute egg → Pop a bit more water in the kettle, and you have yourself a hack for creating a cooked jammy egg for lunch. Place the egg in a saucepan and pour over boiling water. Simmer over medium heat for 7 minutes, then place in a bowl of cold water, and come back to peel it at lunchtime.

Marinate ingredients → Using herbs, different spices and citrus peel, you can marinate various proteins—tofu, chicken, salmon, vegetable, feta, and halloumi— for your lunch. This gives them a further depth of flavor when cooking.

Cook grains ahead → Place your grain, such as couscous or bulgur wheat, in a measuring jug and add a bouillon cube, if you have one. Pour double the amount of boiling water over the top, cover, and leave until lunchtime. Uncover and fluff with a fork. Add a small amount of butter and season with salt and pepper for best results.

Short on time? Soak your vegetables in cold water, then just drain and prep.

Soak ingredients → Some ingredients love a soak and it can actually improve their cooking time later. Short on time for washing vegetables? Soak them in cold water in the sink. Try soaking any grain, rice, or noodle in a bowl of cold water, then when you need to use them, strain, and cook according to the package directions.

Flatten tofu → This hack is for all tofu lovers, and it definitely saves on time. It helps the tofu firm up, making it easier to coat in breadcrumbs, or simply fry it in a pan. Put a clean dish towel on a plate, add the firm tofu on top, and cover with the dish towel. Add a plate and something heavy, such as a can on top to weight it down. Leave until needed.

GETTING AHEAD OF YOUR WEEK

Here is a small but succinct guide on saving time, reducing stress, and ensuring you have nutritious lunches ready to go.

Many of the recipes in this book can be cooked in 15 minutes or less. Some are great for batch cooking, and others may take a little longer. You may not have time to plan ahead, but the one thing you can do is to shop ahead.

01.

PLANNING

CREATE A MEAL PLAN
Have a flick through this book and get an idea of what you'd like to eat for the week. Consider a variety and choose ones that resonate with you. Swap the vegetable or replace the protein, if you prefer. Make it more interesting for you.

MAKE A SHOPPING LIST
Note down what you have run out of and what ingredients you need.

BATCH COOK DISHES
Any batch cooking you'd like to do?

02.

COOKING

MAKE A FERMENT
Make one or two ferments, relishes, dressings, nut or seed mixes, or flavor boosters. (See Chapter 5 for ideas.)

ROAST A VEGETABLE
Whole roast a vegetable to use in your lunches all week. It takes thirty minutes to roast seven to eight whole onions and up to two hours to roast a whole celery root. This helps save time and also brings out the caramelization flavors of the vegetable, adding a layer of complexity to your lunches that you can't get with quick cooking. (See pages 78 to 79 for details.)

It's important to be flexible. Sometimes you might not be in the mood for a particular lunch, so swap it with another day's lunch if you can. Check out the chapter that uses only five ingredients as you will find lots of super-quick lunches.

04.

PREPPING

PREP AHEAD
Cook ahead any grains, beans, pasta, or proteins that might be great to bulk up the lunches for the week. These can be stored in the refrigerator for up to four days.

03.

05.

STORING

CHILL LEFTOVERS
It's important to store leftovers and any other perishable foods in the refrigerator. Most prepared lunches can last three to five days.

FREEZE FOR LATER
You can batch cook four lunches for the month ahead, then eat one a week.

KEEP INGREDIENTS SEPARATE
It's good to keep ingredients, especially salad ingredients, separate and then combine them just before eating to maintain freshness and texture.

PACKING

REUSE JAM JARS
Jam jars are not only plastic free, but they are useful for creating ferments, and for shaking and storing dressings. They fit well in the refrigerator, can be easily labeled (for example, put the date when you made the ferment), and can be easily cleaned in the dishwasher ready for a new batch.

STORING LEFTOVERS
Use airtight containers for leftovers, portions of protein, and stews and soups, which can fit neatly into the refrigerator.

DON'T FORGET YOUR LEFTOVERS

Some people swear by them while others detest them, so which camp are you in? Boiling an extra egg, adding a piece of chicken, roasting extra vegetables, and piling on a few more grains at dinner can create some handy time-savers for lunch the next day.

RECIPES THAT TRANSFORM LEFTOVERS

Japanese Omelet → page 22

Fish Hot Cakes → page 33

Mackerel Egg Fried "Leftover" Rice → page 38

Onion Fried Rice → page 72

Egg on Toast → page 93

Broccoli Bulgur Bowl → page 105

Leftover Rice Soup → page 135

Leftover Chicken and Rice Salad → page 154

HOW TO KEEP YOUR LEFTOVERS INTERESTING

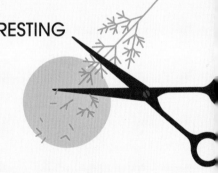

Vary textures → This is where a jar of sauerkraut, a nutty seed mix, or a citrus flavor booster comes into their own. Combine these jars of goodness to add extra flavor to leftovers.

Keep it fresh → Add herbs, greens, or a squeeze of lemon to brighten up and make them taste freshly made.

Mix up the flavors → Use different sauces, dressings, or spices to change the flavor profiles of leftovers. It can make the same base ingredients feel like a completely new dish.

TAKES 15 MINUTES

There are two vital ingredients that you need to create a nourishing meal quickly. One is a pantry you can rely on, and two is a variety of tinned fish you love! Not a fan of fish ... there are vegetable swaps all the way through.

NAAN IT UP

MAKES: 1

1⅓ cups (200 g) red or
   pink tinned salmon,
   drained and any
   bones removed
1 tablespoon olive oil
1 store-bought naan bread,
   about the size of
   your hand
2½ tablespoons ricotta
½ cup (15 g)
   snipped chives
1 tablespoon chili jam or
   1 tablespoon Peanut
   Rayu (page 180) or
   1 tablespoon
   orange marmalade
¼ cucumber, sliced
1 small handful of baby
   spinach leaves

**Otherwise known as a "naanwich," this warm,
crunchy, creamy delight hits all the textures in
just 10 minutes. It's so satisfying!**

Fry the salmon in the olive oil for 5 to 6 minutes until
slightly crispy. Either toast the naan for a few minutes
on one side in the toaster, or dry-fry in a skillet for 2
minutes on each side until warm and slightly crispy.
Lay the naan on a serving plate, spread over the ricotta,
sprinkle with chives, add the crispy salmon, and spoon
over little morsels of chili jam. Place the cucumber and
spinach on top and roll up.

TIP
No naan bread? Use a flatbread. No fish? Swap the
salmon for ½ cup (50 g) cubed feta or 1 cup (50 g)
cooked mushrooms.

TOPPING
Quick Onion Relish (page 179)

TINNED FISH— ARE YOU A FAN?

Tinned fish is a popular pantry ingredient. It's not only convenient, it has longevity, and an amazingly rich nutritional value, being high in omega-3 fatty acids, protein, and various vitamins and minerals.

This staple ingredient is a great way of adding flavor, protein, and healthy fats to a dish. Here are a few ways you can use tinned fish:

Salads → Mix into green salads or potato salads for added protein and flavor.

Sandwiches → Tuna and salmon mix well with mayonnaise, yogurt, or cream cheese to make a spread.

Pasta or noodle dishes → Toss using olive oil, garlic, and herbs for a quick tasty meal.

Casseroles and bakes → Incorporate into casseroles as a main protein.

Stir-fries → A quick protein addition.

Soups and broths → Great in ramen, noodle soups, and seafood soups.

Stuffed vegetables → Perfect with stuffed bell peppers or tomatoes with rice and herbs.

Omelets or frittatas → Tuna, salmon, crab, and mackerel are all good with egg.

HEALTH BENEFITS OF TINNED FISH

Rich in omega-3 fatty acids → Tinned fish like salmon, sardines, and mackerel are packed with omega-3, which are essential for heart health, brain function, and reducing inflammation in the body.

High in protein → Tinned fish is a good source of protein, which is important for muscle growth and repair.

Nutrient dense → Tinned fish is rich in vitamins and minerals such as vitamin D, vitamin B12, selenium, and calcium, which are essential for overall health and wellbeing.

Low in contaminants → They are often lower in contaminants such as mercury compared to larger, predatory fish species.

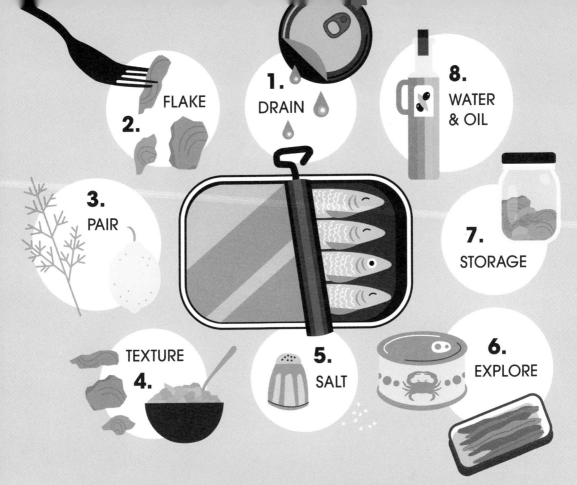

TRICKS ON USING TINNED FISH EFFECTIVELY

1. Drain the liquid → Drain any excess liquid or oil to prevent your dish becoming too wet.

2. Flake it → Break up the fish into flakes with a fork before adding it to recipes like salads or sandwiches.

3. Tinned fish pairs well with → Lemon, garlic, herbs, onion, avocado, and mustard. Experiment with different flavor combinations to see what you enjoy most.

4. Consider texture → Depending on the dish, you may want to preserve the texture of the fish or process it for a smoother consistency.

5. Salt content → Tinned fish can be salty, so be mindful of adding extra salt.

6. Experiment → Explore what you can buy, including tuna, salmon, sardines, anchovies, mackerel, and crab.

7. Storage → Once opened, leftovers should be stored in an airtight container in the refrigerator and eaten within three days.

8. Packed in water and oil → Try to buy fish that's packed in spring water or olive oil. Flavored varieties come with added sodium and sugars.

JAPANESE OMELET

MAKES: 1

2 eggs
1 red chile, seeded
    and sliced
2 scallions, thinly sliced
½ cup (100 g)
    premium crabmeat
1 teaspoon dark soy sauce
½ teaspoon
    Worcestershire sauce
¾ cup (60 g) chopped
    bok choy
½ zucchini, grated
½ tablespoon cornstarch
Juice of ½ lime
1½ ounces (40 g)
    cucumber, halved,
    seeded, and
    thinly sliced
1 tablespoon olive oil
1 teaspoon oyster sauce

A highly flavorful quick lunch, this Japanese omelet packs a punch. It's very versatile, so you can happily swap in any other greens as well as leftover cooked vegetables.

Beat the eggs in a bowl, then add half of the chile, 1 sliced scallion, the crabmeat, soy sauce, Worcestershire sauce, bok choy, zucchini, and cornstarch.

In another bowl, mix the lime juice with the remaining chile, scallion, and the cucumber. Set aside.

Heat the oil in a small skillet and pour in the omelet mixture. Cook for 3 minutes until browned on one side. Flip over and cook for another 3 minutes. Slide out onto a plate and top with the cucumber salad. Drizzle with oyster sauce.

TIP
Not keen on crab? Use smoked mackerel. No fish in the pantry? Use a whole zucchini instead of half.

TOPPINGS
Peanut Rayu (page 180) / Kimchi Slaw (page 160) / Mustard Seed Shallots (page 185)

CASHEW TONNATO WITH GRIDDLED BABY GEM

Prep: 5 min
Cook: 10 min

SERVES: 1 with
enough tonnato
for another
2 tablespoons extra-virgin
olive oil, plus extra
for drizzling
2 oil-packed
anchovy fillets
1 garlic clove
¾ cup (120 g) tinned
tuna, drained
3 tablespoons lemon juice
½ cup (70 g) raw cashews
1 baby gem, cut
into quarters
3 asparagus spears
3 broccoli florets, halved
½ teaspoon hot
pepper flakes
½ tablespoon
capers, rinsed
Salt and black pepper
Bread, toasted, for
serving (optional)

This flavorful sauce can be made ahead and kept in the refrigerator for five days. It's brilliant with any roasted vegetable as it's full of protein.

Blitz the oil, anchovies, garlic, tuna, lemon juice, cashews, and seasoning in a blender until smooth.

Heat a large griddle or skillet until piping hot. Place all the vegetables in a bowl and drizzle with olive oil. Season. Lay the vegetables out on the griddle and cook for 4 to 5 minutes on each side, turning them over as they slightly char. Pour half of the tonnato on a plate and rest the charred vegetables on top. Sprinkle with the hot pepper flakes and capers. Mop up the sauce with toasted bread, if desired.

TIP
Use the tonnato sauce as a base under juicy summer sliced tomatoes or crispy new potatoes.

TOPPINGS
Kimchi Slaw (page 160) / All the Pinks (page 163) / Yellow Zucchini Kraut (page 163) / Za'atar Chickpea Crunch (page 173) / Nutty Pangrattato (page 174)

ANCHOVY PASTA

SERVES: 1

1¾ ounces (50 g) dried
  whole wheat pasta,
  such as spaghetti
  or linguine
3 tablespoons salted
  butter, chopped
2 oil-packed anchovy
  fillets, finely chopped
1 garlic clove, grated
Zest and juice of ½ lemon
1 tablespoon capers, rinsed
1 tablespoon coarsely
  chopped flat
  leaf parsley
Salt and black pepper
Parmesan cheese,
  for serving

A tin of anchovies in your pantry can produce
a lip-smacking, salty, satisfying lunch in minutes.
Follow these directions carefully, and soon you'll
be doing it with your eyes shut!

Cook the pasta in a pot of boiling, salted water
according to the package directions. Drain, setting
2 to 3 tablespoons of the pasta cooking water aside.

Meanwhile, melt the butter in a skillet over medium
heat, add the anchovies, and gently stir, pressing and
breaking them up with a wooden spoon for 3 minutes.
Reduce the heat and add the garlic. After 2 minutes, add
¼ cup (60 ml) pasta cooking water to the pan and whisk
to emulsify. Whisk in the lemon juice and zest, then add
the drained pasta and capers. Cook gently for 2 minutes,
adding the reserved pasta water to loosen. Stir in the
parsley, season well with pepper, and serve with
grated Parmesan.

TIPS
Reheating cooled pasta can change the starch, making it
easier to digest. If you don't feel like pasta today, try using
cannellini beans or lima beans. Add ⅓ cup (80 g) canned
beans with the capers in place of the pasta .

TOPPINGS
Lime and Cilantro Gremolata (page 182) / Nutty
Pangrattato (page 174) / Sicilian Muffuletta (page 185)

SARDINE TARTINE PICCANTE

Prep: 5 min
Cook: 3 min

SERVES: 1

1 large slice of sourdough
  bread or two
  small ones
1 garlic clove, peeled
2 tablespoons extra-virgin
  olive oil
2 medium ripe tomatoes
1 (3-ounce / 85 g) tin
  sardines picante (spicy)
Zest and juice of ½ lemon
2 tablespoons chopped flat
  leaf parsley
Salt and black pepper

Having something on toast is always going to be a speedy lunch, and it's even better when it's full of goodness. This one hits high on the protein stakes, so you don't become hungry within the hour.

Toast the bread until crispy, then immediately rub the garlic over while still warm. Drizzle with olive oil and season with salt. Using a box grater, grate one tomato and spoon this over the toast. Season. Slice the other tomato and lay on top. Place the sardines on top, then add the lemon juice, zest, and parsley. Serve.

TIPS
Add fresh chile for extra spice. If sardines aren't your thing, then use crumbled feta instead.

TOPPINGS
Lime and Cilantro Gremolata (page 182) / Kimchi Slaw (page 160) / Last of the Veg Curtido (page 164) / All the Pinks (page 163) / Everyday Kraut (page 165) / Quick Onion Relish (page 179) / Sicilian Muffuletta (page 185)

WARM SALMON
NORI CAESAR

Prep: 8 min
Cook: 3 min

SERVES: 1

6 anchovy fillets

1 garlic clove

1 egg yolk

2 tablespoons rice vinegar

2 tablespoons extra-virgin
olive oil

½ teaspoon
Worcestershire sauce

2 tablespoons grated
Parmesan cheese, plus
extra for sprinkling

1⅓ cups (200 g) tinned
red or pink salmon

½ romaine lettuce or
1 head baby gem,
separated into
individual leaves

¼-ounce (5 g) nori sheet,
scissored or broken
into bite-size pieces

Black pepper

**Crispy, crunchy, and creamy, this salad does not
disappoint. Don't shy away from using the nori here,
as it gives it a delicious salty crunch.**

Blitz the anchovies, garlic, egg yolk, vinegar, olive oil,
Worcestershire sauce, and Parmesan in a food processor
or blender. It should be quite thick, so scrape down the
sides. Season generously with pepper and give it another
pulse or two. Pour into a bowl and set aside.

Add the salmon to a skillet and fry for 3 minutes,
pressing it down with the back of a wooden spoon, until
crisp. Remove from the heat.

On a plate or bowl, lay out the lettuce leaves, then spoon
over the crispy salmon, drizzle over the dressing, and
sprinkle with nori and more Parmesan.

TIPS

No nori? Add a few nuts for added crunch. Replace the
salmon with chicken or boiled eggs.

TOPPINGS

Nutty Pangrattato (page 174) / Everyday Kraut
(page 165) / All the Pinks (page 163) / Spicy
Pumpkin Mix (page 173)

FISH HOT CAKES

Prep: 6 min
Cook: 16 min

MAKES: 4

1 cup (200 g) leftover
mashed potato
from 1 large to
medium potato
1 (5½-ounce / 160 g) tin
tuna in spring
water, drained
6 anchovy fillets (optional)
1 tablespoon fresh dill or
2 tablespoons dried
Zest of ½ lemon
¼ cup (30 g) cornmeal
or 1 cup (50 g)
panko breadcrumbs
1 tablespoon olive oil
Crisp green salad,
for serving

Leftover mashed potato works wonders here. Alternatively, throw a large potato into the oven at midmorning, then fluffy mash is ready for lunch

Mix the mashed potato, tuna, anchovies (if using), dill, and lemon zest in a bowl, then shape the mixture into four cakes. Dip each side of the cakes into the cornmeal or breadcrumbs to stop them sticking to the pan.

Heat the oil in a skillet over medium to high heat. Once hot, reduce the heat to medium and fry two cakes at a time for 4 minutes on each side. Remove and repeat with the remaining cakes. Serve with a green salad.

TIP
Use any other tinned fish or any other leftovers, such as roasted root vegetables.

TOPPINGS
Sicilian Muffuletta (page 185) / Everyday Kraut
(page 165) / Kimchi Slaw (page 160) / All the Pinks
(page 163) / Yellow Zucchini Kraut (page 163)

NIÇOISE SALMON AND AVOCADO TOASTS

Prep: 10 min
Cook: 7 min

SERVES: 1

1 medium egg
3 ounces (80 g) green
    beans, cut into ½-inch
    (1 cm) slices
1 medium ripe
    tomato, grated
1⅓ cups (200 g) tinned
    salmon, drained
2 tablespoons olive oil
½ tablespoon apple
    cider vinegar
6 cherry tomatoes, halved
2-inch (5 cm) chunk of
    cucumber, halved,
    seeded, and sliced
6 green pitted
    olives, chopped
1 avocado, halved, peeled,
    and pitted
1 gem lettuce, shredded
Salt and black pepper

This high-protein lunch makes good use of a whole avocado.

Pour enough boiling water into a saucepan to cover an egg, then, place the egg carefully into the water and cook for 7 minutes, adding the green beans after 2 minutes. Drain and rinse under cold running water. Set aside.

Add the grated tomato to a bowl with the salmon, oil, vinegar, cherry tomatoes, cucumber, and olives. Season and stir with a fork, breaking up the salmon a little.

Peel the egg and cut in half. Place the avocado halves snugly in a bowl and generously spoon the salmon mix into each circular hole. Pop half an egg on each, and top with the lettuce and green beans.

TIP
To remove a half avocado from its skin, dip a large serving spoon into boiling water, then pick up the avocado half and push the spoon down the side and scoop it out in one swoop.

TOPPINGS
Za'atar Chickpea Crunch (page 173) / Sicilian Muffuletta (page 185) / Kimchi Slaw (page 160)

COUSCOUS TUNA
POKE BOWL

Prep: 10 min

MAKES: 1

⅓ cup (60 g) couscous
(whole wheat
if you can get it)
½ low-sodium vegetable
bouillon cube
½ teaspoon cumin seeds
1½ cups (200 g) tinned
tuna in spring
water, drained
1½ cups (200 g) canned
chickpeas, drained
and rinsed
¼ cucumber, seeded
and sliced
5 cherry tomatoes, sliced
in half
1 scallion, sliced
2 romaine leaves, torn into
bite-size chunks
1 handful of sugar snap
peas, if in season

DRESSING:

¼ cup (60 g) tahini
2 tablespoons lemon juice
2 tablespoons olive oil
1 tablespoon maple syrup
1 teaspoon toasted
sesame oil
¼ teaspoon sea salt

Try using whole wheat couscous, as it's a little kinder to your tummy. Poke bowls are pleasing to the eye and deliver on texture. Experiment with flavors and ingredients and build your own favorite.

Add the couscous to a large bowl, then add the bouillon cube and cumin seeds. Pour in ¼ cup (60 ml) boiling water, stir quickly and cover. Let stand for 10 minutes before fluffing with a fork.

For the dressing, whisk all the ingredients together with 3 tablespoons water until smooth. If it feels a little thick, add some more water.

Assemble all the ingredients in a bowl and drizzle the dressing over the top.

TIP
Use any type of fish here. No sugar snaps? Use frozen edamame beans. Eggs, cheese, and beans are all good additions to increase the protein levels.

TOPPINGS
Peanut Rayu (page 180) / Lime and Cilantro Gremolata (page 182) / Yellow Zucchini Kraut (page 163) / Kimchi Slaw (page 160) / All the Pinks (page 163)

MACKEREL EGG FRIED "LEFTOVER" RICE

Prep: 5 min
Cook: 5 min

SERVES: 1

1½ tablespoons olive oil
1 medium egg, beaten
1 small red chile, seeded
    and chopped
1 scallion, finely sliced
½ garlic clove, grated
1 (4½-ounce / 125 g) tin
    boneless mackerel,
    drained, or fresh
    cooked mackerel
⅓ cup (50 g) cooked rice
    (preferably brown)
⅓ cup (40 g) frozen peas,
    edamame, or sweetcorn
3 tablespoons soy sauce
1 teaspoon sesame oil
1 lime wedge and cilantro
    (optional), for serving

This speedy lunch can use any leftover grain, so try barley, quinoa, spelt, or freekeh.

Heat a small drizzle of the oil in a skillet or wok over medium to high heat. Add the beaten egg and stir for 1 minute until softly scrambled. Remove to a plate.

Add the remaining oil to the pan and cook the chile, scallion, garlic, and mackerel for 1 to 2 minutes. Return the egg to the pan and add the rice and peas. Stir for 1 minute, breaking the rice up with the back of a wooden spoon. Stir in the soy sauce and sesame oil. Serve with cilantro and lime.

TIP

All other fish work well here, or try using broccoli, bok choy, tofu, or chicken instead. You can stir-fry Kimchi Slaw (page 160) or Sicilian Muffuletta (page 185) if there isn't anything else in the refrigerator.

TOPPINGS

Kimchi Slaw (page 160) / All the Pinks (page 163) / Last of the Veg Curtido (page 164) / Peanut Rayu (page 180)

TURMERIC BEAN TARTINE

Prep: 5 min
Cook: 10 min

SERVES: 2

1 tablespoon extra-virgin
    olive oil
½ small onion, minced
2 garlic cloves, grated
¾-inch (2 cm) piece of
    fresh ginger, peeled
    and grated
1 teaspoon
    ground turmeric
1 teaspoon ground cumin
2 tablespoons tomato paste
1 cup (240 ml)
    coconut milk
1 (15-ounce / 425 g) can or
    jar lima beans, rinsed
    and drained
1½ cups (70 g) baby
    spinach, finely
    chopped (optional)
Juice of ½ lime
2 slices of sourdough
    bread, or bread of
    your choice
1 teaspoon hot
    pepper flakes
Salt

**This is a super healthy twist on simple beans on toast.
Mix up the beans to keep it fresh each time you
cook it.**

Heat the oil in a pan and fry the onion for 2 minutes.
Add the garlic and ginger and cook for 1 minute. Add
the spices, then the tomato paste and cook for 1 minute.
Add the coconut milk, lima beans, and spinach and
simmer for 3 minutes. Season with salt, then add the
lime juice and serve topped with the beans and sprinkled
with hot pepper flakes.

TIPS
No beans? Use any kind of bean. This sauce works over
noodles or poured over crispy tofu.

TOPPINGS
Peanut Rayu (page 180) / Turmeric Roasted Mix
(page 170) / Spicy Pumpkin Mix (page 173) / Mustard
Seed Shallots (page 185)

CRAB KRAUT CLUB

Prep: 8 min
Cook: 3 min

MAKES: 2

6 thin slices of bread,
    sourdough, white,
    or brown
½ cup (100 g)
    premium crabmeat
4 pickled
    jalapeños, chopped
3 tablespoons plain kefir
2 teaspoons Sriracha
2 large tablespoons
    Everyday Kraut
    (page 165)
1 good handful of lettuce
Salt and black pepper

IF NO KRAUT, MIX:

2 tablespoons thinly sliced
    white cabbage
5 slices of cucumber
2 tablespoons rice
    wine vinegar
1 teaspoon honey
½ teaspoon fennel seeds

A sandwich of dreams, it's crunchy and spicy with hints of the sea. Get ready to be taken somewhere else for those short minutes you have for lunch.

Preheat the broiler and toast the bread on one side until golden. Mix the crab, jalapeños, kefir, and Sriracha together in a bowl and season. Put one slice of bread, toasted-side down on a cutting board and top with the kraut, then the lettuce. Top with another slice of toast and spread over the crab mix. Add the final slice of toast and secure with a toothpick. Cut into quarters and enjoy.

No kraut? Mix the cabbage, cucumber, vinegar, honey, and fennel seeds together in a bowl.

TIP
No crabmeat? Use salmon or tuna, or if you don't have any fish, then use coarsely mashed chickpeas.

TOPPINGS
A tiny bit of Peanut Rayu (page 180) / Kimchi Slaw (page 160) / All the Pinks (page 163) / Last of the Veg Curtido (page 164)

COCONUT SALMON TURMERIC OMELET

Prep: 5 min
Cook: 16 min

MAKES: 4

1 teaspoon
   ground turmeric
5 eggs
1⅔ cups (400 ml) canned
   coconut milk
1 garlic clove, sliced
1 green chile, seeded
   and chopped
1 small onion,
   finely chopped
¾-inch (2 cm) piece of
   fresh ginger, peeled
   and finely chopped
4 tablespoons vegetable oil
Salt and black pepper
Lime wedges, for serving

SALAD:

1⅓ cups (200 g) tinned
   red or pink salmon
3 scallions, halved, then
   cut lengthwise
4 mint leaves
5 radishes, sliced
2 tablespoons rice vinegar
1 tablespoon lime juice
1 red chile, seeded and
   chopped (optional)

This is an Asian-style omelet rich with coconut milk. There is enough ingredients to make four, so you can batch cook them. Store the cooked omelets in an airtight container, then reheat them for a few minutes in a hot oven.

Mix the turmeric, eggs, and coconut milk together in a bowl. Season. Mix the garlic, chile, onion, and ginger together in another bowl.

Heat 1 tablespoon of the oil in a skillet, add 1 tablespoon of the chile mix, and cook for 1 minute. Add scant ½ cup (100 ml) of the batter to the pan and swirl around to coat. Cook for 2 minutes until golden brown. Cover with a lid and cook for 1 minute, then slide onto a plate and repeat to make three more if batch cooking.

Mix all the salad ingredients together. Serve one or two omelets with the salad piled on top and a lime wedge.

TIP

You can use any fish here or pile on the vegetables instead. Use broccoli, cauliflower, bok choy, chard, and kale. Just cook the chile mix first before adding them.

TOPPINGS

Kimchi Slaw (page 160) / All the Pinks (page 163) / Last of the Veg Curtido (page 164) / Spicy Pumpkin Mix (page 173) / Quick Onion Relish (page 179)

TURKISH EGGS WITH SMOKED MACKEREL

Prep: 5 min
Cook: 8 min

SERVES: 1
2 medium eggs
1 dash of white wine
    vinegar (optional)
½ garlic clove, grated
2 tablespoons extra-virgin
    olive oil
½ cup (120 ml)
    Greek yogurt
½ cup (110 g) tinned
    smoked mackerel
2 teaspoons Aleppo
    pepper or red
    pepper flakes
1 flatbread or sourdough
    bread, for serving

Smoked mackerel comes in many forms. If you can't find it in a tin, try fresh smoked mackerel instead.

Either cook 7-minute boiled eggs (page 116) and remove the shells, or cook the eggs in a small saucepan of water with the vinegar. Bring the water and vinegar to a boil, crack both eggs in, and cook for 5 minutes, or until the white is cooked and the yolk is still runny.

Mix the garlic, 1 tablespoon of the oil, and the yogurt together. Set aside.

Dry-fry the mackerel in a skillet for 1 minute, breaking it up with a wooden spoon. Add the remaining oil and the pepper and fry for 2 minutes until crispy.

Spoon the yogurt over the bottom of a serving bowl, then place both eggs on top. Add the crispy mackerel and serve with bread.

TIP
Use smoked salmon if you don't have any smoked mackerel.

TOPPINGS
Quick Onion Relish (page 179) / Mustard Seed Shallots (page 185) / Kimchi Slaw (page 160)

NOT JUST SARDINES ON TOAST

SERVES: 1

1 slice of bread

Olive oil, for drizzling

2 tablespoons parsley
or 1 tablespoon dried

1 small carrot

1 ounce (30 g) celery root

1 scallion, sliced

1 tablespoon
capers, drained

1 tablespoon
Dijon mustard

Zest of ½ lemon

1 tablespoon lemon juice

1 (3-ounce / 85 g) tin
sardines, drained and
mashed with a fork or
kept whole if small

1 baby gem lettuce,
leaves separated

Salt and black pepper

Tinned sardines come in all sorts of sizes and are all packed with protein, vitamins B12 and D, iron, and calcium. You can even try tinned sardines on gem lettuce instead of toast.

Using the small holes of a box grater, grate the bread onto a small plate. Tip the breadcrumbs into a skillet and drizzle over a little oil. Fry for 2 to 3 minutes until crispy. Season, then add the parsley. Set aside.

Using the larger holes on the grater, grate the carrot and celery root over a bowl. Add the scallion, capers, mustard, lemon zest, and juice. Drizzle with olive oil and mix. Season. Stir through the mashed sardines (if using).

Spoon a tablespoon of salad onto each lettuce leaf, then place a sardine on top if they are small, then sprinkle with breadcrumbs and devour.

TIPS

This is where the box grater comes into its own! If sardines aren't your thing, swap in tuna or salmon or even a mashed boiled egg or feta.

TOPPINGS

Lime and Cilantro Gremolata (page 182) / All the Pinks (page 163) / Spicy Pumpkin Mix (page 173) / Nutty Pangrattato (page 174) / Everyday Kraut (page 165)

PESTO BEANS ON TOAST

Prep: 5 min
Cook: 5 min

SERVES: 2

4 cups (570 g) jarred
  white cannellini beans
  or 1 (15-ounce / 425 g)
  can, drained
2 large or 4 small slices
  of sourdough or
  other bread
1½ cups (70 g) spinach
  leaves, washed
1 cup (35 g) basil leaves
3 tablespoons raw cashews
1 tablespoon tahini paste
1 garlic clove (optional)
2 tablespoons olive oil
Zest of ½ lemon
Salt and black pepper

Cannellini or haricot beans are a great match with pesto. Spinach is used here, but explore using other vegetables, such as beet, sundried tomato, or even leftover roasted carrots in the pesto.

Heat the cannellini beans in a pan over low heat until hot. Season well. Toast the bread.

Blitz the spinach, basil, cashews, tahini, garlic (if using), and the olive oil in a blender to a rough paste. Alternatively, blitz it more if you like it smooth. Add half the pesto to the beans and warm through. Spoon onto the toast and sprinkle with the lemon zest.

TIP
Experiment with other nuts and herbs in the pesto, such as almonds, macadamias, and Brazil nuts, or even a mix. If you want to make a batch pot of pesto, triple the ingredients, pop it in a sterilized jar, and leave a film of light olive oil on top before chilling.

TOPPINGS
All the Pinks (page 163) / Nutty Pangrattato (page 174)

ONE VEGETABLE, THREE LUNCHES

If you put the effort in at the beginning of the week, the rewards you can reap are immense. In this chapter we cover five different vegetables, how to bake them whole, and create three lunches from each.

ROASTING WHOLE VEGETABLES

Discover how to bake a whole vegetable and use it all week for lunches. We have chosen five of our favorites to showcase and produce a wide array of lunch ideas.

EGGPLANTS

Preheat the oven to 400°F (200°C). Poke a few holes in a 2¼-pound (1kg) eggplant and bake for 50 to 60 minutes until slightly shriveled. Cool. Yields: 3 cups (300g) roasted eggplant cubes.

BUTTERNUT SQUASH

Preheat the oven to 425°F (220°C). Bake a 2¼-pound (1kg) squash for 1 hour, or until you can poke a knife through. Cut it in half lengthwise and scoop out the seeds. Peel off the skin and use all the remaining flesh. Yields: 4 cups (820g) roasted squash cubes.

What are the benefits of roasting?

Flavorful → Roasting caramelizes the sugars in the vegetable, intensifying their flavors and adding a subtle sweetness.

Versatile → They are versatile, as you can make soups, salads, and dips, as well as pureeing them with beans to make hummus-style additions.

Less prep → Baking whole vegetables requires minimal prep, making it a convenient cooking method. Simply wash, season, and place in the oven.

CAULIFLOWER

Preheat the oven to 400°F (200°C). Smother a 2-pound (900g) cauliflower in butter. Cover and bake until tender. Preheat the oven to 400°F (200°C). Yields: 3 cups (420g) roasted cauliflower florets.

CELERY ROOT

Preheat the oven to 400°F (200C). Place a 2-pound (900g) celery root on a large sheet of foil and rub with olive oil and salt. Wrap and roast for 2 hours. Yields: 4 cups (620g) roasted celery root cubes.

ONIONS

Preheat the oven to 350°F (180°C). Slice tops off 8 onions (2¼ pounds / 1kg). Place in a dish. Add oil and butter. Season. Bake for 25 minutes. Increase oven to 400°F (200°C) and cook for 15 minutes. Yields: 4 cups (1kg) roasted onions.

Roast the celery root (see pages 78 to 79), then store in a container or covered in the refrigerator for up to four days.

WARM LENTIL, CAPER, AND CELERY ROOT SALAD

Prep: 5 min
Cook: 15 min

SERVES: 1

¼ cup (40 g) brown lentils or ¼ can cooked, drained
1 vegetable or chicken bouillon cube
1 pear, cut in half and cored
1 cup (150 g) chopped roasted celery root (page 55)
1 tablespoon capers, rinsed
1 tablespoon chopped parsley
⅔ cup (30 g) spinach leaves
2 tablespoons French Oomph Dressing (page 177)
1 tablespoon hazelnut pieces, toasted, for serving

A delicious fall salad with a tasty kick of Dijon mustard, this is fresh, crunchy, and packed with protein.

In a pan, cook the dried lentils in ½ cup (120 ml) water with the bouillon cube for 15 minutes, or until tender, then drain. Slice the pear thinly from top to bottom.

Place the lentils, celery root, capers, pear, parsley, and spinach in a large bowl and pour over the dressing. Stir to combine. Serve, sprinkled with hazelnuts.

TIP
No lentils? Try chickpeas or a nutty grain like farro or freekeh.

TOPPINGS
Mustard Seed Shallots (page 185) / Quick Onion Relish (page 179) / Everyday Kraut (page 165) / Za'atar Chickpea Crunch (page 173)

CELERY ROOT AND PULLED MUSHROOM SOUP

Prep: 5 min
Cook: 8 min

SERVES: 1

1 leek, white part only, cut into rings
2 tablespoons olive oil
1 teaspoon thyme leaves or ½ teaspoon dried
1 rosemary sprig or ½ teaspoon dried
1 vegetable or chicken bouillon cube
Scant ½ cup (100 ml) milk or plant milk
7 ounces (200 g) roasted celery root (page 55)
1 king oyster mushroom or 3 oyster mushrooms, cut, pulled, or scraped with a fork into strips
Salt and black pepper

King oyster mushrooms are not only flavorful, they can be super fun to prepare, so grab a fork and shred it into small pieces.

In a saucepan, fry the leek with the thyme and rosemary in 1 tablespoon of the olive oil for 3 to 4 minutes until softened. Add 1¼ cups (300 ml) boiling water to the bouillon cube, then add to the pan together with the milk. Season well. Add the celery root and season, then blitz all the ingredients using a stick blender until combined and thickened.

In another pan, season and fry the mushrooms in the remaining olive oil over high heat for 3 minutes until slightly golden and crispy.

Pour the soup into a bowl and add the mushrooms.

TIP
Fancy more fiber? Add 1⅓ cups (200 g) canned beans to the mix before you blitz. Taste and check the seasoning.

TOPPINGS
Nutty Pangrattato (page 174) / Lime and Cilantro Gremolata (page 182) / Turmeric Roasted Mix (page 170) / All the Pinks (page 163)

ZESTY BEANS WITH CELERY ROOT SMASH

Prep: 6 min
Cook: 8 min

SERVES: 1

⅓ pound (150 g) roasted
    celery root (page 55)
2 tablespoons tahini
3½ tablespoons chicken
    or vegetable stock
½ onion, finely chopped
1 tablespoon olive oil
1 teaspoon grated ginger
1 garlic clove, grated
3 Tuscan kale
    leaves, stripped
½ cup (100 g) cooked
    lima beans, drained
1 tablespoon white
    miso paste
½ teaspoon maple syrup
1 tablespoon
    chopped parsley
1 teaspoon lemon zest
1 teaspoon chopped
    green chile
Salt and black pepper

Celery root whipped with tahini makes a great base for any bean mix or stew. The fresh chile relish finishes the dish perfectly, but if you don't have any then just grate some lemon zest over the top instead.

Blitz the celery root with the tahini and stock until smooth. Season.

Fry the onion in the oil in a skillet for 2 minutes, then add the ginger and garlic. Season and cook for 1 minute. Add the kale and cook for 2 minutes before adding the beans, miso, and maple syrup. It might need a splash of water to loosen. Warm through for 2 minutes.

Mix the parsley, lemon zest, and green chile in a bowl with salt. Spread the celery root smash on a plate, spoon over the beans, and sprinkle the chile mix on top.

TIP
No lima beans? Use chickpeas or any other beans.

TOPPINGS
Peanut Rayu (page 180) / Kimchi Slaw (page 160) / All the Pinks (page 163) / Spicy Pumpkin Mix (page 173) / Za'atar Chickpea Crunch (page 173)

Roast the squash (see pages 78 to 79), then store the flesh covered in the refrigerator for up to four days.

SPICED SQUASH AND FETA PATTIES

Prep: 5 min
Cook: 6 min

MAKES: 3

4 ounces (120 g)
    roasted squash
    (page 54)
½ cup (60 g) cubed feta
2 scallions, finely sliced
Juice of ½ lemon
1 tablespoon garam masala
1 egg
1 tablespoon chopped
    cilantro or parsley
1 red chile,
    seeded and finely
    chopped (optional)
1¾ tablespoons
    all-purpose flour
2 tablespoons olive oil
    for frying
Salt and black pepper
Creamy Green Kefir
    Dressing (page 179),
    and leafy salad
    for serving

This satisfying lunch is ready in under 15 minutes. What's not to love?

Place all the ingredients, except the flour and olive oil, in a large bowl. Season and stir to combine. Using your hands, create three large balls. Spread the flour out on a plate, then press down each ball using the palm of your hand to make a patty.

Heat the oil in a large skillet and fry the patties for 2 to 3 minutes until golden. Flip over carefully and cook on the other side for another 2 to 3 minutes. Serve with the dressing and a leafy salad.

TIPS
Omit the chile and add more fresh herbs. Add chickpeas for added fiber.

TOPPINGS
Peanut Rayu (page 180) / Mustard Seed Shallots (page 185) / Spicy Pumpkin Mix (page 173)

WINTER PANZANELLA SQUASH SALAD

Prep: 8 min
Cook: 8 min

SERVES: 1

1 slice of sourdough or
   ciabatta, cut into cubes
2 tablespoons extra-virgin
   olive oil
6 Brussels sprouts,
   finely sliced
2 kale leaves, preferably
   Tuscan kale, torn
½ cup (115 g)
   chopped roasted
   butternut squash
   (page 54)
¼ cup (20 g) shaved
   Parmesan cheese
1 tablespoon
   pomegranate seeds
1 to 2 tablespoons Apple
   Cider Dressing
   (page 177)
Salt and black pepper

There is some prep to do here to get you in the lunch zone. If you don't have any pomegranate seeds then add some chopped dried apricots instead.

Preheat the oven to 425°F (220°C). Toss the bread cubes in 1 tablespoon of the oil and season. Bake in the oven for 8 minutes, or until golden and crispy.

In a skillet, fry the sprouts and kale in the remaining oil for 2 to 3 minutes. Season.

Place all the ingredients, except the bread, in a bowl and pour over the dressing. Spoon onto a plate and add the crispy bread.

TIP

For a gluten-free alternative, crisp some chickpeas by baking in the oven for 12 minutes in oil or in an air fryer heated to 400°F (200°C) for 5 minutes. You can also cook the bread in an air fryer heated to 400°F (200°C) for 4 to 5 minutes.

TOPPINGS

Za'atar Chickpea Crunch (page 173) / Nutty Pangrattato (page 174) / Lime and Cilantro Gremolata (page 182)

SQUASH AND CURRY LEAF DAL

Prep: 5 min
Cook: 15 min

SERVES: 2

½ cup (100 g) red
lentils, washed
1 garlic clove, sliced
¾-inch (2 cm) piece of
fresh ginger, peeled
and sliced
½ red onion, sliced
1 tablespoon coconut oil
or olive oil
6 to 8 curry leaves, fresh
or dried
½ teaspoon fennel seeds
¼ pound (115 g) roasted
butternut squash
(page 54)
1⅔ cups (80 g) spinach
leaves, washed
Salt and black pepper

FOR SERVING:

2 tablespoons plain yogurt
1 green chile, sliced
1 tablespoon cashews,
toasted (optional)
1 cup (30 g) cilantro
(optional)

**This comforting bowl holds its flavor for several
lunches if you want to batch cook it. Just double or
treble the quantities and freeze in individual portions.**

Cook the lentils in a pan with twice as much water for
15 minutes. Most of the liquid will be absorbed; don't
drain. Season well once cooked.

Meanwhile, in a skillet, fry the garlic, ginger, and red
onion in the oil for 2 minutes. Add the curry leaves and
fennel seeds and cook for another 2 minutes. Season.

Add the onion mixture to the lentils, then add the squash
and spinach and stir through to combine. Season. Serve
in bowls with the yogurt, chile, cashews, and cilantro.

TIP

Add chard or other soft greens for extra fiber and beans
for extra goodness.

TOPPINGS

Peanut Rayu (page 180) / Kimchi Slaw (page 160) / All
the Pinks (page 163) / Lime and Cilantro Gremolata
(page 182)

Roast the onions (see pages 78 to 79),
then peel off the skins and store covered
in the refrigerator for four days.

ROASTED ONION SOUP
WITH TAHINI CROUTONS

Prep: 5 min
Cook: 10 min

SERVES: 1

1 tablespoon olive oil

1 tablespoon butter

1 garlic clove, sliced

1 cup (200 g) sliced
roasted onions
(page 55)

1 small thyme sprig or
½ teaspoon dried

½ tablespoon white
miso paste

1 cup (240 ml) chicken or
vegetable stock

1 slice of sourdough
or ciabatta

1 tablespoon tahini

**Having roasted onions ready speeds up this delicious
soup and doesn't disappoint on flavor.**

Heat the oil and butter in a skillet over medium heat and
fry the garlic for 1 minute. Add the onions and thyme
and cook for 1 minute. Add the miso, then pour in the
stock. Simmer for 5 to 6 minutes.

Meanwhile, toast the bread and preheat the broiler. Once
the bread is toasted, spread the tahini over the top, then
broil for 2 minutes. Transfer the toast to a cutting board
and cut into cubes.

Pour the soup into a bowl and top with the croutons.

TIP

No bread? Crisp up some chickpeas in a pan with a
spoonful of tahini for 5 minutes.

TOPPING

Za'atar Chickpea Crunch (page 173)

BLUE CHEESE, BEET, AND ONION TART

Prep: 5 min
Cook: 14 min

MAKES: 1

1 (13-ounce / 375 g) package ready-rolled puff pastry sheet
1 small or ½ large roasted onion, sliced (page 55)
1 small beet, peeled and grated
1 teaspoon maple syrup
½ teaspoon thyme leaves, or pinch of dried
1 teaspoon sherry vinegar
¼ cup (30 g) crumbled blue cheese, such as Gorgonzola or other favorite
1 tablespoon extra virgin olive oil
⅛ cup (20 g) walnut pieces
Salt and black pepper

Crispy, creamy, and salty, this tart hits all the satisfying spots for lunch. Serve with salad, if desired.

Preheat the oven to 425°F (220°C). Line a baking sheet with baking parchment.

Cut the pastry sheet in half, then in half again; this is a good portion for one. Double the ingredients to make two. Mix the sliced onion and grated beet in a bowl with the maple syrup, thyme, and vinegar. Season. Lay the pastry on the lined baking sheet. Spoon the onion mixture into the middle of the tart, leaving a ¾-inch (2 cm) border. Crumble the cheese on top and drizzle with a little oil.

Fork around the edge of the tart and bake for 14 minutes until the cheese has melted and the pastry is golden and crispy. Crumble over the walnuts and serve with salad.

TIPS
Great served with sliced fennel, cucumber, and gem lettuce covered in French Oomph Dressing (page 177). If you are not into beet, try using jarred artichokes.

TOPPINGS
Lime and Cilantro Gremolata (page 182) / Nutty Pangrattato (page 174)

ONION FRIED RICE

Prep: 5 min
Cook: 10 min

SERVES: 2

2 tablespoons toasted
  sesame oil

1 carrot, grated

½ zucchini, grated

¾-inch (2 cm) piece of
  fresh ginger, peeled
  and sliced

1¼ cups (250 g) cold
  cooked brown rice

1 roasted onion, sliced
  (page 55)

1¼ cups (150 g)
  frozen peas

2 eggs, beaten (optional)

2 to 3 teaspoons soy sauce
  or tamari

1 red chile, chopped with
  seeds for hot, removed
  for mild

1 tablespoon black
  sesame seeds

**This is a simple dish for a simple day. Use whatever
rice you have—leftover basmati, jasmine, or long grain
rice; it all works here.**

Heat 1 tablespoon of sesame oil in a large skillet over
medium heat and fry the carrot, zucchini, and ginger for
5 minutes until tender not mushy. Add the rice, onion,
and peas and cook for 4 minutes. Push the rice to the side
of the pan, add the remaining oil, and crack in the eggs, if
using. Prod it around the pan until it is just set. Break up
the egg and stir through the rice. Drizzle the tamari over
the top and serve with chile and sesame seeds.

TIPS

No rice? Use a grain, such as spelt, quinoa, or bulgur
wheat. No veg? Use a kraut or kimchi and stir through.

TOPPINGS

Peanut Rayu (page 180) / Kimchi Slaw (page 160) / Last
of the Veg Curtido (page 164) / All the Pinks
(page 163) / Everyday Kraut (page 165)

ONE VEGETABLE, THREE LUNCHES

Roast the eggplant (see pages 78 to 79), then store in a lidded container in the refrigerator for up to four days.

WARM EGGPLANT SALAD WITH WHIPPED FETA

Prep: 5 min
Cook: 5 min

SERVES: 1

2 tablespoons butter
1 tablespoon olive oil
1 garlic clove, sliced
6 cherry tomatoes
1 (2¼-pound / 1kg)
    roasted eggplant,
    skin removed (page 54)
3 tablespoons chickpeas
1 ounce (30 g) feta
3 tablespoons plain yogurt
Zest of ½ lemon
1 tablespoon
    chopped parsley
Salt and black pepper
Toast, crackers, grissini,
    or flatbreads, for
    serving (optional)

If you are looking for some home-cooked food that makes you feel good, here's today's lunch sorted.

Heat the butter and oil in a skillet. Add a pinch of salt, then add the garlic and fry for 30 seconds. Add the tomatoes and cook for 2 minutes. Add the eggplant and chickpeas and stir-fry for 2 minutes. Season.

Whisk the feta and yogurt in a bowl until combined. Add the lemon zest and whisk again until smooth.

Spoon the warm eggplant mix into a bowl and add the whipped feta on top. Sprinkle with parsley. Scoop up with toast, crackers, grissini, or flatbread, or eat with a spoon.

TIP
Farro or barley would be a good addition here to add more fiber.

TOPPING
Mustard Seed Shallots (page 185)

ONE VEGETABLE, THREE LUNCHES

BERBERE EGGPLANT
WITH HUMMUS

Prep: 5 min
Cook: 12 min

SERVES: 1

1 tablespoon olive oil
½ garlic clove, grated
1 teaspoon grated ginger
1 tablespoon berbere
  spice mix
8 cherry tomatoes,
  coarsely chopped
1 jarred roasted red bell
  pepper, sliced
1 (2¼-pound / 1kg)
  roasted eggplant,
  skin removed (page 54)
1 mild red chile, seeded
  and chopped
1 tablespoon maple syrup
1 tablespoon tamari or
  soy sauce
1½ cups (200 g)
  chickpeas, rinsed
1 tablespoons tahini
Juice of ¼ lemon
Salt and black pepper
Flatbread, for serving

A warm spiced stew with smooth, silky mash. No
chickpeas? Use pasta, rice, beans, or a simple flatbread.

Heat the oil in a skillet and fry the garlic and ginger
for 1 minute. Add the berbere spice and cook for 30
seconds. Add the tomatoes and red pepper and cook for
5 minutes until the tomatoes start breaking down. Add
the eggplant, chile, maple syrup, and tamari and cook for
2 minutes so all the ingredients are combined.

Blitz the chickpeas, tahini, and lemon juice in a blender
with 1½ tablespoons cold water. Season and blitz again.
Warm the hummus in a pan for 1 to 2 minutes, then
spoon into a bowl. Add the eggplant mixture on top and
serve with a flatbread.

TIP
Try a mix of quinoa and brown long grain rice instead of
the chickpeas.

TOPPINGS
Quick Onion Relish (page 179) / Turmeric Roasted Mix
(page 170) / Nutty Pangrattato (page 174)

BABA GANOUSH TOASTS WITH GREEN BEAN SALAD

Prep: 5 min
Cook: 8 min

SERVES: 1

1¾ ounces (50 g) flat
    beans/runner or string
    beans, each cut into
    3 pieces
2 tablespoons extra-virgin
    olive oil
1 scallion, cut into 3 pieces
¼ cup (30 g)
    edamame beans
Juice of ½ lemon
1 flatbread or pita
⅓ pound (150 g) roasted
    eggplant, skin removed
    (page 54)
1 teaspoon sesame oil
1 tablespoon finely
    chopped mint and/or
    parsley or pinch
    of dried
Pinch of sesame seeds
Salt and black pepper

**Charred flat beans have a great texture and
marry well with the soft smokiness of a
slow-cooked eggplant.**

Season the flat beans with 1 tablespoon of the olive oil
and salt. In a griddle pan or skillet, cook the beans for
2 to 3 minutes on each side, until charred and cooked
through. Add the scallion for the last 3 minutes.

Cook the edamame beans in a pan of boiling water for
2 minutes, then drain. Add to a bowl with the lemon
juice and remaining olive oil. Add the warm beans and
scallion and season. Griddle or toast the bread and
spread the eggplant over. Drizzle with sesame oil and top
with the beans, herbs, and sesame seeds.

TIP
Add fine green beans or frozen peas to increase the fiber.

TOPPINGS
Peanut Rayu (page 180) / Everyday Kraut (page 165)

Roast the cauliflower (see pages 78 to 79), then store in a lidded container in the refrigerator for up to four days.

CAULIFLOWER TOASTS

Prep: 5 min
Cook: 8 min

SERVES: 1

1 tablespoon extra-virgin olive oil

1½ cups (170 g) coarsely chopped roasted cauliflower (page 55)

¼ cup (60 g) cottage cheese

½ cup (30 g) grated Parmesan, plus 1 teaspoon extra for topping

¼ cup (25 g) grated cheddar

1 salted anchovy fillet, chopped

½ teaspoon Dijon mustard

1 large or 2 small slices of sourdough, or other favorite bread

Few snips of chives

Salt and black pepper

Raw cauliflower is perfect for freezing so coarsely chop 12 ounces (340g) of raw cauliflower and freeze half of it for another time.

Preheat the broiler. In a bowl, mix the oil with the cauliflower, all cheeses, anchovy, and mustard. Season. Lightly toast the bread in a toaster or under the broiler. On a baking sheet, lay out the toast and spoon over the cauliflower mix generously. Broil for 3 to 4 minutes until bubbling and slightly golden. Serve sprinkled with chives and a good grinding of black pepper and the 1 teaspoon Parmesan.

TIP
If anchovies aren't your thing, try chopping a few sundried tomatoes or olives to add an umami kick.

TOPPINGS
Everyday Kraut (page 165) / All the Pinks (page 163) / Kimchi Slaw (page 160) / Peanut Rayu (page 180) / Turmeric Roasted Mix (page 170)

SPICED CAULIFLOWER ON WHIPPED HUMMUS

Prep: 5 min
Cook: 10 min

SERVES: 1

1 tablespoon olive oil

½ red onion, sliced

½ garlic clove, sliced

1 teaspoon mustard seeds

½ teaspoon cumin seeds

⅓ pound (150 g)
    roasted cauliflower
    (page 55)

1 (15-ounce / 425 g) can
    cannellini beans,
    rinsed and drained

Zest of ½ lemon

1 tablespoon tahini

2 tablespoons chopped
    cilantro or ½ teaspoon
    coriander seeds

Salt and black pepper

A warming bowl of goodness that's full of fiber and spices to heat up the body on a cold day.

Heat the oil in a skillet over medium to low heat and cook the onion, garlic, and spices for 3 to 4 minutes. Add the cauliflower and season. Reduce the heat to low and cook for another 2 to 3 minutes.

For the hummus, blitz the beans, lemon zest, tahini, cilantro, and 1½ tablespoons cold water in a blender until smooth. Season well and blitz again. Pour into a small saucepan to heat for a few minutes, then spoon half into a bowl. Add the cauliflower mix on top.

TIP

Use other beans or even lentils to make the hummus. Mix it up and find a favorite.

TOPPINGS

Peanut Rayu (page 180) / Kimchi Slaw (page 160) / Quick Onion Relish (page 179) / Lime and Cilantro Gremolata (page 182) / Turmeric Roasted Mix (page 170)

CAULIFLOWER TACOS WITH AVOCADO CREAM

Prep: 5 min
Cook: 5 min

MAKES: 3

1 tablespoon olive oil
⅓ pound (150 g) roasted
   cauliflower, cut into
   bite-size pieces
   (page 55)
½ teaspoon paprika
¼ teaspoon ground cumin
½ cup (30 g) thinly sliced
   red cabbage
½ small red onion, thinly
   sliced in half-moons
1 tablespoon
   chopped jalapeños
1 teaspoon apple
   cider vinegar
3 tortillas
1 ripe avocado, pitted
   and peeled
Juice of ½ lime
2 pink radishes,
   thinly sliced
Salt and black pepper

This speedy lunch can come together in minutes.
Spice up the cauliflower as much as you want.

Heat the oil in a pan and cook the cauliflower, paprika,
cumin, and a pinch of salt for 2 to 3 minutes so it's warm
through and the spices are releasing their aroma.

Add the cabbage, onion, and jalapeños to a bowl. Drizzle
with a little vinegar and mix. Toast the tortillas or dry-fry
them in a skillet on each side for 20 seconds.

Blitz the avocado, a pinch of salt, and the lime juice in a
small food processor or blender. Spread a large spoonful
of avocado on each tortilla, then add some spiced
cauliflower, red cabbage slaw, and the radishes.

TIP
No avocado? Blitz yogurt with cilantro and lime juice for
a simple green sauce.

TOPPINGS
Peanut Rayu (page 180) / Kimchi Slaw (page 160) / All
the Pinks (page 163) / Quick Onion Relish (page 179) /
Creamy Green Kefir Dressing (page 179)

ONE VEGETABLE, THREE LUNCHES

ONLY FIVE INGREDIENTS

When the pantry is bare, creating a dish that is nutritionally balanced and tasty is still possible. This chapter teaches you to adapt to what you have. No long ingredient lists, just a few alternatives await.

SALTY EGG PASTA

SERVES: 1

2 eggs, beaten

1 tablespoon olive oil, plus extra for drizzling

½ onion or scallion, minced

½ teaspoon red pepper flakes or hot pepper flakes

½ teaspoon mixed dried herbs or a few fresh leaves of sage/parsley or cilantro

⅓ cup (25 g) grated Parmesan or any cheese, such as feta, cheddar, or halloumi

Salt and black pepper

When there isn't much food in the house, this is my go-to "pasta" dish. All you need are two eggs, a bit of hard cheese, and a few spices.

Beat the eggs in a bowl with 2 tablespoons water. Heat the oil in a medium skillet over medium heat and cook the onion for 1 to 2 minutes until softened. Add the red pepper flakes and herbs to the beaten egg and season. Reduce the heat to low and pour the egg mixture over the onion. Swirl gently before letting it cook evenly for 2 minutes. No prodding or moving it at this stage. Loosen the omelet gently around the edges, then slide it out onto a cutting board. Cut into ½-inch- (1 cm)-width long strips or thick noodles and serve in a bowl with the cheese sprinkled on top and a drizzle of olive oil.

TIP
As the omelet is so thin, it only needs to be cooked on one side and no prodding. Simple.

TOPPINGS
Quick Onion Relish (page 179) / Kimchi Slaw (page 160) / Last of the Veg Curtido (page 164) / Yellow Zucchini Kraut (page 163) / All the Pinks (page 163) / Everyday Kraut (page 165) / Mustard Seed Shallots (page 185)

SMOKED SALMON ON SMASHED CHICKPEAS

Prep: 6 min

SERVES: 1

1½ cups (200 g) canned
    chickpeas, drained
    and rinsed

1 tablespoon extra-virgin
    olive oil, plus extra
    for drizzling

2 cornichons or cucumber
    pickles, sliced

2 teaspoons tahini

Juice of ½ lemon

1 slice of bread, lettuce
    leaf, or cracker

4 ounces (120 g)
    cured smoked salmon

Salt and black pepper

This delicious salad can be served on your favorite cracker, slice of sourdough, on a baby gem lettuce, or on a rice cake. Grab what you have and serve this filling lunch on top.

Either use a potato masher or the back of a wooden spoon to mash about 75 percent of the chickpeas in a bowl with the oil. Add a chopped cornichon.

Mix 1 tablespoon water, the tahini, and lemon juice together in another bowl. Season and stir through the chickpea mixture.

To assemble, choose your vessel, either bread, lettuce, or cracker, then spoon on the mashed chickpeas, add the remaining whole chickpeas, flake over the salmon, and top with the remaining cornichon and an extra drizzle of olive oil.

TIP
Swap smoked trout for smoked mackerel. No fish?
Use feta.

TOPPINGS
Lime and Cilantro Gremolata (page 182) / Spicy Pumpkin Mix (page 173) / Kimchi Slaw (page 160) / Last of the Veg Curtido (page 164) / All the Pinks (page 163) / Creamy Green Kefir Dressing (page 179)

EGG ON TOAST

SERVES: 1
Olive oil
1 medium or large egg
1 slice of bread, toasted
Salt and black pepper

OPTION 1
3 sage leaves
¼ teaspoon hot
    pepper flakes
1 teaspoon lemon rind

OPTION 2
1 tomato diced
¼ teaspoon cumin seeds
¼ teaspoon mustard seeds

OPTION 3
5 curry leaves
1 teaspoon lime rind
3 tablespoons chickpeas

OPTION 4
1 slice of chopped ham
¼ cup (20 g) chopped hard
    cheese and sauerkraut

OPTION 5
½ onion, diced
½ red bell pepper, diced
Sherry vinegar

This recipe is not really a recipe, it's more a list of ideas to create your ideal egg on toast. Use your pantry, herbs, and leftovers and see what you can come up with.

Add 1 tablespoon of oil to a small skillet and fry your first chosen ingredient. Let sizzle and cook for 1 minute. Now add your next ingredient and crack an egg on top. Fry over low to medium heat for 2 minutes. Season and cook until all the egg white is cooked through before adding the last ingredient. Cook for 30 seconds. Remove the pan from the heat, drizzle olive oil over the toast, and lay your egg with all its flavors on top.

TIPS
Crack an egg into a small cup or jar before adding it to the pan. It lowers the breakage rate tenfold. Use either sourdough bread or your own favorite bread.

ZESTY BEAN QUESADILLAS

Prep: 5 min
Cook: 5 min

SERVES: 1

1 (15-ounce / 425 g) can
    mixed beans, rinsed
    and drained
½ tablespoon red
    wine vinegar
½ teaspoon hot
    pepper flakes
1 medium tortilla
3 tablespoons
    grated cheddar
Salt and black pepper

These quesadillas are warm, comforting, and ready in minutes. Feel free to use a flatbread if you don't have any tortillas.

Mix the beans, vinegar, and hot pepper flakes together in a bowl. Season. Heat a skillet over medium heat and lay out the tortilla. Spoon the bean mixture on one half of the tortilla and sprinkle with the cheese. Fold in half and cook for 1 minute. Flip over and cook for another 2 to 3 minutes until golden and the cheese has melted.

TIPS

Use any canned beans here. No cheddar? Use your favorite hard cheese.

CRISPY HALLOUMI WITH MASHED AVOCADO

SERVES: 1

1 tablespoon olive oil

1 teaspoon ground cumin or ½ teaspoon cumin seeds

3 slices of halloumi

1 avocado, peeled and pitted

Juice of 1 lime

1 whole wheat pita

Salt

This recipe can take a lot of different toppings, depending on your mood. Check out the tips and topping list below and find your favorite.

Heat the oil in a medium skillet, add the cumin and sizzle for 30 seconds. Add the halloumi and fry for 8 to 10 minutes, flipping over halfway through, making sure it's crispy and golden on each side.

In a bowl, mash the avocado and half of the lime juice with the back of a fork. Season with salt. Heat the pita in a dry skillet over high heat for 30 seconds on each side or pop it into a toaster.

To assemble, lay the pita flat on a plate, spoon over the avocado smash, then top with the crispy halloumi. Squeeze the rest of the lime juice on top.

TIP

Replace the halloumi with chickpeas, crumbled cauliflower, sliced bell peppers, or cubed zucchini.

TOPPINGS

Mustard Seed Shallots (page 185) / Lime and Cilantro Gremolata (page 182) / Peanut Rayu (page 180) / Kimchi Slaw (page 160) / Turmeric Roasted Mix (page 170) / All the Pinks (page 163) / Quick Onion Relish (page 179)

TURKEY TACOS

Prep: 5 min
Cook: 5 min

SERVES: 1

¼ cup (50 g) ground
    turkey or chicken
1 garlic, grated
1 scallion, sliced
1 medium tortilla or
    2 mini tortillas
1 tablespoon oil
1 teaspoon sesame seeds
Salt and black pepper

This speedy taco lunch is bursting with flavor.

In a bowl, mix the turkey with garlic and scallion. Season well. Using the back of a spoon or your fingers, spread the mixture onto the tortilla, patting it as flat as you can.

Heat the oil in a skillet over medium heat. Lay the tortilla, meat-side down, and cook for 4 minutes, or until the meat has browned and is crispy. Flip over and cook for 1 minute. Remove from the pan using a spatula. Sprinkle with sesame seeds.

TIP
No ground meat? Use a single pork, chicken, or turkey sausage, squeezing out the mix, or try a mix of grated halloumi and Parmesan. Are the sausages already flavored? If not, add a few more herbs.

TOPPINGS
Peanut Rayu (page 180) / Quick Onion Relish (page 179) / Za'atar Chickpea Crunch (page 173) / Lime and Cilantro Gremolata (page 182)

98   ONLY FIVE INGREDIENTS

POTATO AND EGG WRAP

Prep: 5 min
Cook: 9 min

SERVES: 1

1 medium potato, cut into small cubes

1 tablespoon olive oil

3 slices of halloumi, cut into small cubes

¾ cup (40 g) spinach leaves, chopped

2 eggs, beaten

1 medium whole wheat tortilla

Salt and black pepper

Hungry? This ought to do it! Adapt the recipe to what you have in the refrigerator, and serve alongside a small salad or sliced avocado if you have it.

Using a medium skillet, cook the potato in the olive oil for 2 minutes. Season. Add the halloumi and cook for another 2 minutes, or until crispy. Add the spinach, then the eggs, and season. Cook for 4 minutes. Place the tortilla on top, then flip the tortilla over with a spatula or cover with a dinner plate, and flip so that the egg is facing up. Cook for 1 minute, fold the tortilla over, and serve, cut into wedges.

TIP
Swap the spinach for tomatoes or bell peppers and add grated cheese in the beaten egg for extra cheesiness.

TOPPINGS
Kimchi Slaw (page 160) / Peanut Rayu (page 180) / Everyday Kraut (page 165) / All the Pinks (page 163) / Quick Onion Relish (page 179)

GREEN BEAN TAHINI TARTINE

Prep: 5 min
Cook: 5 min

SERVES: 1

⅓ cup (75 g) plain yogurt

⅛ cup (40 g) tahini paste

1 tablespoon olive oil

3½ ounces (100 g) green
    beans, trimmed

½ teaspoon hot
    pepper flakes

Salt and black pepper

1 slice of sourdough
    or bread, toasted, or
    a cracker, for serving

Feel free to use broccoli or zucchini here instead of the beans, or try all three as a mix.

Whisk the yogurt and tahini together in a bowl and season. Set aside.

Heat a skillet over medium heat, add the oil, green beans, and hot pepper flakes and season. Cook for 3 to 4 minutes until bright green and slightly crispy. Remove from the heat. Spread the tahini yogurt mix on the toast or cracker and lay the beans on top.

TIP

Add your favorite chopped herbs for added fiber, and 1½ cups (200 g) cooked lima or cannellini beans to the tahini mix for a heavier lunch option.

TOPPINGS

Turmeric Roasted Mix (page 170) / Peanut Rayu (page 180) / Last of the Veg Curtido (page 164) / Za'atar Chickpea Crunch (page 173) / Nutty Pangrattato (page 174) / Lime and Cilantro Gremolata (page 182)

ONLY FIVE INGREDIENTS

BROCCOLI BULGUR BOWL

Prep: 5 min
Cook: 12 min

SERVES: 2

¼ cup (50 g) bulgur wheat
½ large (6 ounces / 170 g)
   crown broccoli, thick
   stem removed
1 small onion, minced
1 tablespoon olive oil, plus
   extra for drizzling
1 cup (30 g) herbs, mint,
   parsley, and/or basil
1 lemon, juiced and
   ½ zested
Salt and black pepper

This delicious bowl of goodness is perfect for leftovers. Add cheese, fish, meat, and extra nuts, depending on what you have in your pantry and your mood.

Cook the bulgur wheat according to the package directions. Season well.

Blitz the broccoli in a food processor to very small pieces. In a skillet, cook the onion in the oil for 2 minutes until softened. Add the broccoli crumbs and cook for another 2 minutes. Place everything in a bowl along with the herbs and lemon zest and juice. Drizzle with extra olive oil to finish.

TIPS

Use other grains like couscous, rice, or spelt. Try blitzing up other root vegetables like this to speed up cooking time. This is also a perfect dish for any leftovers you might have.

TOPPINGS

Turmeric Roasted Mix (page 170) / Last of the Veg Curtido (page 164) / Everyday Kraut (page 165) / Spicy Pumpkin Mix (page 173)

KOREAN SCALLION PANCAKE

MAKES: 1

1 cup (120 g)
   all-purpose flour
3 tablespoons cornstarch
2 teaspoons miso paste
1 teaspoon gochugaru
   flakes or hot
   pepper flakes
1 tablespoon olive oil
8 scallions, sliced
   lengthwise down the
   middle and cut in half

Try this pancake dipped into any kind of spicy sauce, or smothered in Peanut Rayu (page 180) for a tasty kick. Serve with a salad.

In a large bowl, mix the flour, cornstarch, miso, and gochugaru with scant 1 cup (200 ml) water to make a smooth batter. Heat the oil in a skillet over medium heat, add the scallion pieces, then add the batter and tilt the pan gently until the batter covers the bottom of the pan. Fry for 2 minutes. Flip over and fry for another 2 to 3 minutes. Keep flipping until the pancake is crispy.

TIP
Use edamame peas, chard, spinach, or other soft vegetables here if you want to increase your fiber.

TOPPINGS
Kimchi Slaw (page 160)

SHOPPING TO CREATE A BALANCED MEAL

To be able to make a healthy, satisfying lunch, it's good to have a few essential items in the pantry and refrigerator. These need to be on the weekly or monthly shopping list whether you shop in store or online, have a regular delivery.

WHAT IS A HEALTHY LUNCH?

The ideal balanced lunch provides the necessary nutrients and energy to support your health. Equally important, a healthy lunch regulates your hunger, so you're less prone to snacking in the late afternoon. Take these things into account when planning:

1. Protein → Protein builds and repairs body tissues and makes you feel fuller. For protein choose chicken, turkey, tofu, eggs, beans, fish, or cheese.

2. Whole grains → High in fiber and more filling than refined carbs, whole grain options include whole grain pasta, farro, rice, and bread.

3. Fruits and vegetables → Fill half your plate with fruits and veg to pack in vitamins, minerals, and fiber.

4. Healthy fats → Found in foods like nuts, seeds, avocados, and olive oil. Healthy fats are essential for brain function.

5. Hydration → A balanced lunch has plenty of hydration. Include drinks such as water or herbal tea.

From this chapter, you can discover that making a simple lunch with just five ingredients is possible using a mix of pantry essentials with a few fresh foods sprinkled through.

SETTING UP A WEEK OF LUNCHTIME SUCCESS

It can be tempting to skip meal planning when you are working from home. The fact that you can pop into the kitchen and throw a meal together or make lunch on the fly, can sometimes lead to bad choices unless you have planned a week of lunches you want, and have ordered the items you need.

WHOLE GRAINS
½ cup (55 g) cooked grains or 1 slice of bread

DAIRY
1 cup (225 g) yogurt or 1½ ounces (40 g) cheese

PROTEIN
3 to 4 ounces (80 to 115 g / palm of your hand) chicken or 3 tablespoons beans

HEALTHY PLATE GUIDELINES

HEALTHY FATS
½ avocado, ¼ cup (30 g) nuts, 1 to 2 tablespoons seeds, 1 tablespoon olive oil

VEGETABLES
2 cups (150 g) leafy salad green or 1 cup (75 g) cooked vegetables

FRIED ZUCCHINI WITH WHIPPED TOFU

Prep: 15 min
Cook: 8 min

SERVES: 1

1 (10½-ounce / 300 g)
   package extra-firm tofu
Juice of 1 lemon, plus a
   little grated lemon zest
   for garnish
⅓ cup (40 g) sundried
   tomatoes, drained
1 zucchini, cut in
   half lengthwise
1 tablespoon olive oil
1 tablespoon
   pistachios, chopped
Salt and black pepper

This dish is creamy, flavorful, and ready in minutes. Blitzing tofu is a super quick way of adding protein.

Press the tofu using a dish towel with a plate on top for 10 minutes to extract any excess liquid. Add to a blender with ½ teaspoon salt and 2 tablespoons lemon juice and blitz until smooth. Add the sundried tomatoes and pulse a few more times.

Run a knife in a crisscross pattern over each zucchini half, trying not to go through the skin. Season. Sear in a skillet with the oil for 4 minutes on one side until golden. Flip over and sear on the other side for 3 to 4 minutes until cooked through. Test with a sharp knife; it should be soft but hold its shape.

Serve the whipped tofu with the zucchini on top. Sprinkle with pistachios and grate over a little lemon zest.

TIP
Explore with other ingredients, such as fresh herbs, scallions, or leftover vegetables.

TOPPINGS
Turmeric Roasted Mix (page 170) / Spicy Pumpkin Mix (page 173) / Nutty Pangrattato (page 174) / Mustard Seed Shallots (page 185)

MUSHROOM AND SHALLOT TART

Prep: 5 min
Cook: 25 min

SERVES: 1

1 sheet of ready-rolled puff pastry

2 medium cremini mushrooms, sliced

1 tablespoon olive oil

1 small shallot, thinly sliced

2 tablespoons cottage cheese

1 egg, beaten

Are you short on time? Then whip up this easy mushroom tart in just 30 minutes.

Preheat the oven to 375°F (190°C). Lay the puff pastry out on wax paper and cut out 3¼ by 6¼-inch (8 by 16 cm) rectangle. Roll the pastry back up, cover, and chill in the refrigerator for later.

In a skillet, fry the mushrooms in a little olive oil, so they are slightly browned, and water has been released. Drain on paper towels.

Lay the mushrooms on some wax paper so they cover roughly 3¼ by 6¼-inches (8 by 16 cm), then spread the shallots and cottage cheese on top of the mushrooms. Lay the pastry on top, pushing down the edges with a fork. Brush the tart with beaten egg and bake for 20 minutes, or until golden. Let cool for a few seconds before carefully flipping over. When flipping the tart over, if you feel that the topping needs a little more cooking, return it to the oven for a couple of minutes.

TIP

No mushrooms or shallots? Spinach, chard, and scallions are all good options. Try other soft cheeses, if you prefer.

TOPPING

Everyday Kraut (page 165)

ONLY FIVE INGREDIENTS

CHANA DAL FRITTERS

Prep: 5 min
Cook: 12 min

MAKES: 10

1 cup (200 g) chana
 dal (yellow) lentils
1 tablespoon coconut oil
 or olive oil, plus extra
 for frying
10 curry leaves
2 garlic cloves
1 green chile
1 teaspoon fennel seeds

These lentils can be soaked in the refrigerator overnight, or pop them in a bowl of water at breakfast time and they will be ready for lunch. Serve on their own or with cucumber and plain yogurt.

Soak the lentils in a bowl of water for 3 to 4 hours. Drain and rinse.

In a small skillet, heat the coconut oil and fry the curry leaves for 2 minutes, or until crispy. Add to a blender with the garlic, chile, and fennel seeds and blitz until the mixture comes together. It should be quite coarse. Transfer to a bowl.

Heat the oil for frying in a skillet. Add a large tablespoon of the mixture to the skillet and press down slightly using the back of the spoon. Add another 3 tablespoons of the batter and leave a gap between them. Cook until crisp on one side, then flip over and cook for another 2 to 3 minutes. Remove and repeat until all the mixture is used.

TIP
These fritters are perfect for using up any leftover vegetables such as spinach. Add a fried onion and more spices, if desired. Fry a few more curry leaves in oil when frying the fritters and stir them through yogurt to serve.

TOPPINGS
Quick Onion Relish (page 179) / All the Pinks (page 163) / Mustard Seed Shallots (page 185)

JAMMY EGG SALAD

Prep: 5 min
Cook: 8 min

SERVES: 1

2 large eggs

Scant ½ cup (100 ml) plain
or Greek yogurt

½ avocado, peeled, pitted,
and sliced

5 cherry tomatoes, halved

3 thick slices of cucumber,
cut into chunks

1 tablespoon extra-virgin
olive oil

Salt and black pepper

Toast, crackers, chili
oil, or seeds, for
serving (optional)

**This salad is based on Turkish-style eggs. It is a quick
go-to lunch with endless possibilities to create your
own style.**

Place the eggs in a saucepan and cover with boiling water.
Simmer for 7 minutes. Have a bowl of ice water at the
ready. When the eggs are cooked, transfer them to the ice
water for 2 minutes to stop them cooking. Peel and rinse
under cold water to remove any shell. Set aside.

Add the yogurt to a serving bowl and season. Arrange
the avocado, tomatoes, and cucumbers on top and season
again. Cut the eggs in half and lay these on top. Drizzle
with olive oil and season with salt. Serve with toast or
crackers, some chili oil, or seeds for extra crunch.

TIP

Jammy eggs can be made ahead and stored in the
refrigerator for up to three days.

TOPPINGS

Turmeric Roasted Mix (page 170) / Quick Onion
Relish (page 179) / Nutty Pangrattato (page 174) / Spicy
Pumpkin Mix (page 173) / Creamy Green Kefir Dressing
(page 179) / Apple Cider Dressing (page 177) / Peanut
Rayu (page 180) / Kimchi Slaw (page 160) / Everyday
Kraut (page 165)

ONLY FIVE INGREDIENTS

SIMPLE
LUNCH
BOWLS

Soups, broths, salads, stews, and beans, this chapter is full of hearty dishes that nourish and warm the soul, packing in as much fiber and nutrients as possible.

GREEN CHICKPEA STEW WITH RICOTTA

Prep: 5 min
Cook: 16 min

MAKES: 2

3½ ounces (100 g) kale, preferably Tuscan

¾ cup (40 g) spinach leaves

⅓ cup (10 g) parsley, stalks included

2 tablespoons extra-virgin olive oil

½ white onion, finely chopped

4 garlic cloves, grated

5 cups (700 g) jarred chickpeas or 2 (15-ounce / 425 g) cans

Zest and juice of ½ lemon

1 red chile, seeded and finely chopped

2 heaping tablespoons ricotta

1 tablespoon grated Parmesan

Salt and black pepper

Bread, for serving

You can use dried, canned, or jarred chickpeas in this dish, but my personal preference is to use a jar, as they are tastier. If you don't have any ricotta, then use any other soft cheese instead.

Blanch the kale, spinach, and parsley in a large pan of boiling water for 2 minutes. Drain and submerge in cold water for a few minutes. Squeeze out the water and blitz in a blender with 1 tablespoon of the olive oil. Season and add a little water if it needs loosening.

In a skillet, cook the onion in the remaining olive oil for 4 minutes. Add the garlic and cook for 2 minutes. Add the chickpeas and their brine, and the green sauce and cook for 8 minutes. Season with salt.

Pour into a bowl, add the lemon juice, zest, chile, and ricotta. Sprinkle with Parmesan and serve with bread.

TIPS

Use any bean you like here. No beans? Swap with a whole wheat pasta shape. This sauce is also delicious over small potatoes.

TOPPINGS

Peanut Rayu (page 180) / Lime and Cilantro Gremolata (page 182) / Nutty Pangrattato (page 174)

SIMPLE LUNCH BOWLS

CANNELLINI CACIO E PEPE WITH A CRUMB

Prep: 5 min
Cook: 10 min

SERVES: 2

2 garlic cloves

1 tablespoon extra-virgin olive oil, plus extra for drizzling

1 rosemary sprig

5 cups (700 g) jarred cannellini beans or 2 (15-ounce / 425 g) cans, drained and rinsed

1½ cups (350 ml) stock or water

½ stick (60g) butter, cubed

2 teaspoons ground black pepper

¾ cup (60 g) finely grated pecorino or Parmesan or mix of both

This dish is a potential weekly lunch for cheese lovers. You can change it up by adding a different topping each time.

Bash the garlic with a rolling pin, keeping the skin intact. Add the olive oil to a large saucepan and fry the garlic and rosemary for 2 minutes. Discard the rosemary. Add the beans and stock or water and cook gently for 3 minutes. Add the butter on top, letting it melt before adding the pepper. Shake the pan as it cooks. Add the cheese, waiting for it to melt before shaking and stirring to emulsify everything.

Pour the beans into a bowl. Add a topping and an extra drizzle of olive oil to finish.

TIPS

No cannellini beans? Use lima or haricot beans.

Stir through some spinach or Tuscan kale.

Important tip: Do not shake the pan until everything is melted to make sure it emulsifies.

TOPPINGS

Kimchi Slaw (page 160) / Peanut Rayu (page 180) / Za'atar Chickpea Crunch (page 173) / Mustard Seed Shallots (page 185)

ONE AND ONLY STOCK

Prep: 10 min
Cook: 20 min

MAKES: about 12 cubes, depending on the size of ice-cube tray or one 12-ounce (350 g) jar
3 carrots, coarsely chopped
2 leeks, chopped
¼ celery root, peeled and diced
1 onion, quartered
4 garlic cloves
3 celery stalks, chopped
5 cherry tomatoes or 1 medium tomato, chopped
2 cups (60 g) parsley, stalks included
3½ tablespoons sea salt
Olive oil, for topping (optional)

This is a bonus recipe that acts as a great base for most of the recipes in this chapter. Master this, and the colder months of lunch will become pure joy!

Blitz the carrots, leeks, and celery root in a blender. Push the ingredients down the sides and add the remaining ingredients. Blitz again, then pulse until wet and smooth. Pour into an ice-cube tray and freeze for 1 hour. Alternatively, pour into a sterilized jar, pour a layer of olive oil on top, so it is covered, and leave in the refrigerator for up to 2 to 4 weeks.

To make 4 cups (1 L) stock, fry 3 ice cubes in 2 tablespoons butter over low heat for 7 to 8 minutes so the flavors infuse. Add 4 cups (1 L) boiling water, then simmer for 10 minutes. It's ready for use.

TIP
Change the flavor of the stock depending on what's in the refrigerator, and what season it is. Play around with salt levels using seaweed, such as nori and kelp, or dried mushrooms. Tamari sauce can give a saltier depth, but also more tomatoes can give it a more rounded feel, just make sure they are ripe.

ULTIMATE BONE BROTH

Prep: 5 min
Cook: 2¼ hrs

MAKES: 6 portions

2¼ to 2¾ pounds
(1 to 1.25 kg)
chicken carcasses

2¼ pounds (1 kg) pork
neck and back bones

1 yellow onion

3 scallions, just the
green parts

1¼-inch (3 cm) piece
of fresh ginger

3 garlic cloves

1 piece of kelp (optional)

This is not quite a Tonkotsu ramen broth, which takes 14 hours, but is a fabulous pork and chicken bone broth that you can easily do at home. It freezes well, and your gut will love you.

Blanch the chicken and pork bones in a pot of boiling water for 20 minutes, then drain and clean under cold running water.

Place the bones and the remaining ingredients in a stock pot with 4.2 quarts (4 L) water. Bring to a boil, removing any scum that floats to the top. Reduce the heat, cover, and simmer for 2 hours. Add to the Ramen recipe on page 128.

MAKING AN EVERYDAY RAMEN

Ramen, the famous Japanese noodle soup, originally from China, has ventured into kitchens worldwide. Known for its meat or fish stock base and a myriad toppings, this soup is so versatile and a super choice for your lunch repertoire. Use different noodles, vegetables, sauces, and toppings, and your ramen brings on a taste of its own.

Top tips for making a ramen

Choose the noodles → You want to use fresh or dried ramen noodles for good results. If wheat isn't your thing or you want to mix it up, try using rice or buckwheat noodles as options.

Make a flavorful broth → If you haven't got time to make the bone broth, creating ramen with vegetable or chicken stock is great for a speedy lunch. Add flavors like miso, teriyaki, nori, bonito flakes, charred leek, ginger, and garlic to add a quick depth of flavor.

Add toppings → These are almost as important as the stock. Customize your ramen with your favorites from soft-boiled eggs, bamboo shoots, corn, and scallions.

Balance flavors → Try to achieve a harmonious balance of flavors by adjusting the saltiness, sweetness, and umami levels by adding soy, mirin, tahini, miso, or rice wine to the broth.

Cook ingredients separately → Cook each component of your ramen separately to ensure they're cooked to perfection. This includes the noodles, protein, and vegetables.

HEALTH BENEFITS OF RAMEN

Good for adding protein → Protein is essential for muscle repair and growth. Pork, chicken, tofu, and eggs are all good sources.

Noodles → Cook with whole wheat or buckwheat to provide more fiber.

Vegetables → Spinach, mushrooms, and scallions, provide essential vitamins, minerals, and antioxidants that support overall health.

Soups or broths → These are a good source of hydration.

YOUR ONE NOODLE SOUP

Prep: 5 min
Cook: 20 min

SERVES: 1

1 cup (240 ml) dashi
  or vegetable stock
1 cup (240 ml)
  vegetable stock
2 tablespoons dried
  mushrooms, chopped
¾-inch (2 cm) piece of
  fresh ginger, peeled and
  cut into matchsticks
2 ounces (60 g) noodles,
  preferably soba
1 egg
3 tablespoons tamari sauce
3 cremini
  mushrooms, sliced
1 baby bok choy, chopped
2 scallions, chopped
2 teaspoons sweet white
  miso paste
1 teaspoon toasted
  sesame oil
1 chile, seeded
  and chopped

**If you like your soups and love Asian flavors, this is
the soup for you. It's ready in 25 minutes.**

Place the dashi and vegetable stock in a saucepan with
a lid. Add the dried mushrooms and ginger, cover, and
bring to a simmer for 15 minutes.

Cook the noodles in a pan of boiling water for 4 minutes,
or according to the package directions.

In another pan, pour in enough boiling water to cover an
egg. Add 2 tablespoons of the tamari sauce, then lower
in the whole egg and simmer for 7 minutes. Pop the egg
into a bowl of cold water to stop it cooking.

Add the cremini mushrooms, bok choy, and scallions to
the stock and simmer for 3 minutes. Uncover, add the
remaining tamari and the miso and stir until the miso
has dissolved. Remove from the heat. Peel the egg and cut
in half. Pour the soup into a bowl, add the noodles, egg, a
drizzle of sesame oil, and the chile.

TIP
Try adding salmon or smoked mackerel for extra protein.
Tofu works well too.

TOPPING
Peanut Rayu (page 180)

SIMPLE LUNCH BOWLS

SPRING BEAN STEW

Prep: 5 min
Cook: 15 min

SERVES: 3, good
    for batch cooking
2 tablespoons extra-virgin
    olive oil
1 small onion, minced
1 garlic clove, minced
2¾ cups (700 ml)
    vegetable stock
    (2 homemade vegetable
    stock ice cubes,
    page 124)
1 (15-ounce / 425 g) can
    cannellini beans, rinsed
    and drained
¾ cup (100 g) chopped
    green beans
⅓ cup (50 g) chopped
    runner or
    string beans
¾ cup (100 g) frozen peas
3 radishes, sliced
4 asparagus, sliced into
    ½-inch (1 cm) circles
1 handful of basil
    leaves, torn
Zest of 1 lemon
Salt

As the outside temperature warms up a little, it's time to seek out green beans at their best. Take this soup to the next level and grate some lemon zest over the top just before serving.

Heat the oil in a pan and fry the onion and garlic with a pinch of salt for 4 minutes, or until softened. Add the stock and all the beans and simmer for 4 minutes. Stir in the peas, radishes, and asparagus and simmer for another 4 minutes. Serve with torn basil leaves and grated lemon zest.

TIP
If you don't have all these vegetables, increase the ones you do have. Add more peas or even sliced fennel.

TOPPINGS
Za'atar Chickpea Crunch (page 173) / Lime and Cilantro Gremolata (page 182) / Sicilian Muffuletta (page 185) / Yellow Zucchini Kraut (page 163)

ROMESCO SOUP

Prep: 5 min
Cook: 12 min

SERVES: 6, good for
  batch cooking
1 cup (120 g) raw almonds
4 garlic cloves, peeled
4 jarred roasted
  bell peppers
1 (15-ounce / 425 g) can
  peeled plum tomatoes,
  juice drained
2 tablespoons apple
  cider vinegar
1 teaspoon
  smoked paprika
1 tablespoon maple syrup
  or pinch of sugar
2 cups (480 ml) vegetable
  stock (3 homemade
  vegetable stock
  ice cubes, page 124)
Salt and black pepper
Chopped herbs (optional),
  for garnish

Smoky roasted bell peppers in a jar can become an essential pantry item for a working week. Add it to your regular shop if this soup hits the spot.

Dry-fry the almonds in a skillet over medium heat for 4 to 5 minutes until slightly golden. Add the garlic for the last 30 seconds. Transfer to a blender, add the peppers, tomatoes, vinegar, smoked paprika, and syrup and blitz for 1 minute to a coarse sauce. Season and add half of the stock and blitz again until smooth. Pour into a saucepan and add the remaining stock. Bring to a low simmer before serving with a soft chopped herb, if using.

TIPS
If you have any roasted vegetables left over, such as sweet potato, squash, onions, and tomatoes, blitz them in the blender too for added fiber. Swap the almonds with cashews and sunflower seeds for a variation.

TOPPINGS
Za'atar Chickpea Crunch / Nutty Pangrattato (page 174) / Peanut Rayu (page 180) / Lime and Cilantro Gremolata (page 182)

SIMPLE LUNCH BOWLS

LEFTOVER RICE SOUP

Prep: 5 min
Cook: 15 min

SERVES: 1
FOR BASE:
2 tablespoons olive oil
1 garlic clove, sliced
¾-inch (2 cm) piece
    of fresh ginger, peeled
    and sliced
2 scallions, cut into
    ¾-inch (2 cm) slices
1½ cups (160 g) leftover
    cooked rice
1 teaspoon miso paste
1 cup (240 ml)
    vegetable stock

FOR TOPPING:
¼ zucchini
1 tablespoon sesame oil
1 anchovy fillet
1 egg yolk
Peanut Rayu (page 180)

This is a quick recipe for a comforting rice-style soup, otherwise known as congee. Often eaten for breakfast in China, it's great to use as a quick base for lunch too. Just add something salty, such as miso, to create a flavorful soup. Top the congee with smoked mackerel, spinach leaves, or fried mushrooms, if desired.

Heat the olive oil in a pan over medium to high heat and fry the garlic, ginger, and scallions for 1 to 2 minutes until golden. Add the rice, miso, and stock. Bring to a boil, then simmer for 12 minutes until thick and soupy. Spoon into a bowl.

For the topping, using a peeler, shred the zucchini into ribbons. Fry in a very hot skillet in the sesame oil with the anchovy. Cook for 1 to 2 minutes, then add to the congee. Add an egg yolk on top, and a drizzle of peanut rayu.

TIP
Leftover chicken, salmon, or tuna work well. Nuts and seeds bring added crunch.

TOPPINGS
Mustard Seed Shallots (page 185) / Za'atar Chickpea Crunch (page 173) / Spicy Pumpkin Mix (page 173) / Kimchi Slaw (page 160)

INSTANT POT SOUP

SERVES: 1

1¾ ounces (50 g)
   glass noodles
1 tablespoon olive oil
¾-inch (2 cm) piece of
   fresh ginger, peeled
   and sliced
1¼ cups (300 ml)
   vegetable or chicken
   stock (1 homemade
   vegetable stock
   ice cube, page 124)
2 tablespoons
   teriyaki sauce
1 teaspoon sesame oil
1 teaspoon maple syrup
   or sugar
½ cup (40 g) sugar
   snap peas, halved
⅓ cup (40 g) frozen peas
   or edamame beans
1 bok choy, cut into
   small chunks

**FOR TOPPING
(OPTIONAL):**

1 tablespoon
   cilantro leaves
1 tablespoon sesame seeds

**If you are short on time, assemble all the dry
ingredients in advance, then just add stock when you
are ready to eat. It's an instant pot noodle at home.**

Soak the noodles in cold water for 10 minutes,
then drain.

Heat the oil in a pan and cook the ginger for 1 minute.
Add the noodles, half of the stock, teriyaki sauce, sesame
oil, and maple syrup. Bring to a boil, then simmer for 5
minutes. Add the vegetables and remaining stock and
simmer for another 3 minutes. Remove from the heat,
add the toppings. Eat straight from the pan or pour into
a bowl.

TIPS

If glass noodles are not for you, use egg or soba, but
adjust the cooking times accordingly. You make this soup
for later using a 17-ounce (500 ml) glass jar. Just add the
noodles to the bottom of the jar and pop the vegetable
ingredients on top. Add hot stock and toppings when you
are ready to eat.

TOPPINGS

Peanut Rayu (page 180) / Quick Onion Relish (page 179)

GARDEN UMAMI SALAD

Prep: 8 min
Cook: 10 min

SERVES: 1

1 soft-boiled egg
1 handful of broccoli
    florets, halved
1 handful of green
    beans, leave tail on
1 handful of snow peas
1 handful of sugar snap
    peas, halved
⅛ cup (15 g) frozen peas
⅛ cup (15 g) frozen
    edamame beans
¾ ounce (20 g)
    dill, chopped

BASE MIX:

2 tablespoons tahini
1½ cups (200 g) canned
    cannellini beans
2 tablespoons olive oil
½ teaspoon salt

DRESSING:

3 tablespoons sesame oil
1 tablespoon soy sauce
1 tablespoon sesame seeds
1 teaspoon honey

This garden salad can be easily changed up depending on the season. You don't need all the dressing so set the rest of the dressing aside for another time.

Add all the dressing ingredients to a jam jar, seal, shake, and set aside. Shake before using.

Cook the egg in a pan of boiling water for 6 minutes. Transfer the egg to a bowl of cold water, then peel. Add the broccoli and green beans to the simmering water and cook for 4 minutes, then drop into cold water. Remove the pan from the heat and add all the peas and edamame beans. Defrost for 3 to 4 minutes.

Blitz all the base mix ingredients with 2 tablespoons water in a blender until smooth. Loosen with a little water if needed, then spoon into a salad bowl.

Drain the peas and beans. Place all the vegetable ingredients in a bowl, mix, then add to the salad bowl. Drizzle half the dressing over the salad and sprinkle with dill.

TIP
Don't have all the vegetables? Just increase the ones you do have. Sliced cabbage, Brussels sprouts, and kale with frozen vegetables works well in winter.

TOPPINGS
Kimchi Slaw (page 160) / Everyday Kraut (page 165) / Spicy Pumpkin Mix (page 173)

CELERY ROOT NOT-QUITE REMOULADE

Prep: 8 min
Cook: 5 min

SERVES: 1

½ small radicchio, leaves pulled and torn

⅓ pound (150 g) celery root, peeled and cut into matchsticks

½ cup (125 g) ricotta

1 small bunch of parsley and / or chives, coarsely chopped

DRESSING:

1½ teaspoons multigrain mustard

3 tablespoons extra-virgin olive oil

1 tablespoon balsamic vinegar

2 dried dates, pitted and finely chopped

1 tablespoon grated lemon zest

This salad is savory and nutty. It has a few extra flavors and more pops of goodness than a normal remoulade.

Simmer all the dressing ingredients, except the lemon zest, in a pan over low heat until the dates have melted, about 4 minutes. Remove from the heat and add the lemon zest. Set aside.

To serve, place the torn radicchio on the bottom of a bowl and sprinkle the celery root over the top. Scoop a teaspoon of ricotta straight from the pot onto the top of the salad and repeat five more times evenly over the salad. Add a topping, if desired. Finally, add 1 to tablespoons of water to loosen the dressing, then drizzle it over the top. Sprinkle with chopped parsley.

TIPS

No dates? Use 1 teaspoon honey or maple syrup for sweetness. Grate the celery root if you are short on time. No toppings? Fry a handful of nuts in a mix of turmeric and ground cumin with honey and a pinch of salt.

TOPPINGS

Turmeric Roasted Mix (page 170) / Nutty Pangrattato (page 174) / Creamy Green Kefir Dressing (page 179) / Quick Onion Relish (page 179)

CITRUS CRUNCH SALAD

Prep: 10 min

SERVES: 1 to 2

½ grapefruit, peeled
   and thinly
   sliced horizontally
1 small orange, peeled
   and thinly
   sliced horizontally
Generous 1 cup (65 g)
   very thinly sliced
   red cabbage
½ cup (35 g) very thinly
   sliced fennel bulb
1 medium beet,
   ends trimmed
1 handful of watercress,
   arugula, or corn salad

DRESSING

Juice of 1 lime
1 tablespoon red
   wine vinegar
3 tablespoons olive oil
1 small hot chile, finely
   sliced (optional)
4 mint leaves,
   finely shredded
½ tablespoon honey

This refreshing salad is crunchy and full of flavor. Use the slicing side of a box grater or a mandoline to slice the cabbage and fennel very thinly.

Add all the dressing ingredients to a jam jar, seal, and shake to emulsify. Set aside.

Add all the salad ingredients to a bowl and pour over the dressing. Mix well before serving.

TIPS

Slicing on a cutting board in the sink helps when preparing beet. For a fall vibe, thinly slice some cauliflower, broccoli, or kohlrabi.

TOPPINGS

Turmeric Roasted Mix (page 170) / Nutty Pangrattato (page 174) / Apple Cider Dressing (page 177) / Creamy Green Kefir Dressing (page 179) / French Oomph Dressing (page 177) / Kimchi Slaw (page 160)

WARM HALLOUMI SALAD WITH ALMONDS

Prep: 5 min
Cook: 14 min

SERVES: 1

2 tablespoons olive oil

4½-ounce (125 g) block
of halloumi, cut
into small chunks

Generous ¾ cup (50 g)
broccoli florets, halved

2 dried dates, pitted
and chopped

¼ cup (30 g) whole
blanched almonds,
coarsely chopped

1 cup (50 g) finely
chopped chard leaves,
stems thinly sliced

1 cup (50 g) torn
kale leaves

1⅔ cups (80 g)
spinach leaves

1 quantity of Apple Cider
Dressing (page 177)

Salt and pepper

Sweet, salty, crunchy, and delicious, this dish hits all the right spots.

Heat 1 tablespoon of oil in a skillet and fry the halloumi until golden and crispy on one side, 3 to 4 minutes. Flip over and fry on the other side until crispy. Spoon onto a plate and set aside.

Add the remaining oil to the pan and add the broccoli. Season with salt and cook for 3 to 4 minutes until sizzling and starting to char. Add the dates and almonds and cook for another minute. Add all the leaves and chard stems. Season again and cook for 4 to 5 minutes until the spinach, chard, and kale have wilted and everything is warmed through.

Tip into a bowl, sprinkle over the halloumi, and drizzle over the dressing. Season with pepper and serve.

TIP

Just use spinach. Frozen spinach is fine; add a few more minutes to the cooking time.

TOPPINGS

Quick Onion Relish (page 179) / Spicy Pumpkin Mix (page 173) / Nutty Pangrattato (page 174) / Lime and Cilantro Gremolata (page 182)

ULTIMATE CHOPPED SALAD

Prep: 8 min

MAKES: 1 to 2

½ head romaine lettuce

5 gherkins

1 scallion

3 cauliflower florets

2 tablespoons
    dried cranberries

1 avocado

1 ball of burrata

1 tablespoon pistachios

1 tablespoon dill fronds

Salt and black pepper

DRESSING:

1 tablespoon pickle brine

1 tablespoon white
    wine vinegar

3 tablespoons olive oil

There's nothing like doing a little knife "workout" at lunchtime to get your brain rebooted. Try out this salad with all the chop chop skills. Once you get into a rhythm you'll be flying.

This salad is fun to chop altogether on a large board. Hold a sharp knife at both ends, working it like a seesaw, and chop away at the ingredients. Chop chop chop away, leaving the burrata to one side. Chop for a good 4 to 5 minutes. Once the ingredients are chopped into small pieces, tip into a bowl. Make a small well in the middle and add the burrata. Whisk all the dressing ingredients or shake in a jam jar and pour over the top. Season with salt and pepper.

TIPS

No burrata? Use cottage cheese or mozzarella. Swap the cauliflower for cabbage or Brussels sprouts. Hate chopping? Blitz the ingredients a few times in a blender.

TOPPINGS

Apple Cider Dressing (page 177) / French Oomph Dressing (page 177) / Creamy Green Kefir Dressing (page 179) / Spicy Pumpkin Mix (page 173) / Turmeric Roasted Mix (page 170) / Nutty Pangrattato (page 174) / Lime and Cilantro Gremolata (page 182)

BUILDING A SALAD

It can be useful to think about building a simple salad through a series of steps. Here are some basic principles that you can follow, then hopefully you will feel confident enough to improvise.

1. Choose your greens → Lettuce / arugula / kale / spinach/ watercress

2. Add a variety of vegetables → Chop and add some colorful vegetables, and even some fruit, such as tomatoes, cucumbers, bell peppers, carrots, radishes, zucchini, cabbage, beet, celery root, apples, pears, nectarines, watermelon, and more.

3. Include protein → To make your salad a little more filling, add some protein. This includes broiled chicken, tofu, eggs, avocado, beans, and cheese.

4. Add texture → Texture is a great way of creating a satisfying salad. Try adding nuts, seeds, or a mix of both, or crispy croutons, a broken crispy taco, crispy chickpeas, or even a panko-style crumb.

5. Include beans or grains → Consider adding a grain or blitzing a bean to create a puree or dip. Or add some dried fruit like cranberries, raisins, or dates for sweetness.

6. Top with dressing → Finishing the salad is important! Citrus, spicy, nutty, or creamy, there are lots of flavors to tap into when creating a dressing.

CREATE A HEALTHY SALAD HABIT:

Pick a base → Choose nutrient-dense vegetables, such as dark leafy greens and mixed greens as the foundation for your salad. Greens are packed with vitamins, minerals, and fiber.

Add color → Incorporate a colorful mix of vegetables, such as tomatoes, cucumbers, bell peppers, carrots, radishes, etc. These add crunch and freshness.

Incorporate flavors → Season with herbs and spices, including basil, cilantro, mint, and dill, as these enhance the flavor of your salad.

Be sure to hydrate → Make sure to stay hydrated. Enjoy your salad with a glass of water or unsweetened herbal tea to stay hydrated and support digestion.

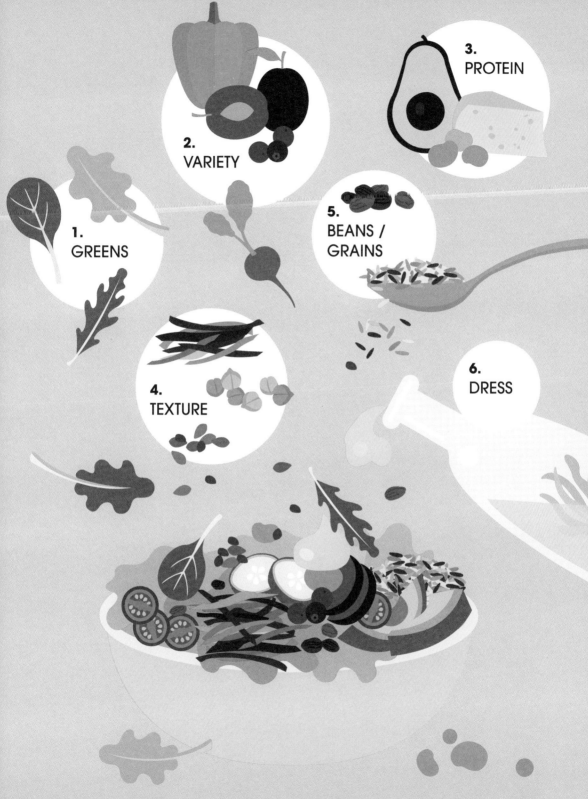

1.
GREENS

2.
VARIETY

3.
PROTEIN

4.
TEXTURE

5.
BEANS /
GRAINS

6.
DRESS

WINTER PURPLE SALAD

Prep: 9 min

SERVES: 2

1½ cups (80 g) thinly
   sliced red cabbage
2 medium beets, grated
2 apples, grated leaving
   the core and skin on
½ red onion, sliced
   on grater
1 quantity of French
   Oomph Dressing
   or Apple Cider
   Dressing (page 177)
Olive oil, for drizzling
1 tablespoon walnut pieces
1 tablespoon chopped
   parsley or
   ½ tablespoon dried

HUMMUS:

1 (15-ounce / 425 g) can
   chickpeas, rinsed
   and drained
Juice of ½ lemon
1 tablespoon tahini
Pinch of salt

Preparing a beet can be a turn off at lunch … spraying its juice over the kitchen counter. Try making this salad on a cutting board in the sink as grating the beet with utter abandonment gives you a sense of freedom.

Place all the vegetables and the apples in a large bowl and pour over the dressing. Stir through and let stand for 5 minutes.

Blitz all the hummus ingredients in a food processor until smooth but still thick. If you need to loosen it a little, then add some cold water.

Spoon half of the hummus onto one side of a salad bowl and drizzle with olive oil. Using tongs, pick up half the vegetable / fruit mix and place it on the other side of the bowl. Sprinkle over the walnut pieces and parsley to finish.

TIPS
No apple? Try a pear or even pomegranate seeds. No chickpeas? Try another bean like cannellini, or a lentil. Mix it up by adding a different herb such as mint or basil.

TOPPINGS
Za'atar Chickpea Crunch (page 173) / Lime and Cilantro Gremolata (page 182) / Quick Onion Relish (page 179)

NOODLE AND EDAMAME SALAD

Prep: 10 min
Cook: 5 min

SERVES: 1

1¾ ounces (50 g) soba noodles

1 carrot, julienned or ribboned

½ white cabbage, thinly sliced

4 radishes, sliced

¼ cup (30 g) frozen edamame beans

¼ cup (30 g) frozen peas

2 scallions, finely sliced

1 tablespoon raw peanuts

1 small bunch of cilantro with stalks, finely chopped

SATAY DRESSING:

2 tablespoons smooth peanut butter

Juice of 1 lime, plus extra for serving

1 teaspoon grated ginger

1 tablespoon tamari sauce

½ tablespoon sesame oil

½ tablespoon maple syrup

1 pinch of salt

This salad brings Thai flavors to your lunch. Defrost the edamame beans and peas in a bowl of warm water before using.

Place the noodles in a pan, pour over boiling water, and cook according to the package directions, about 5 minutes. Strain and pour over cold water. Tip the noodles into a large bowl.

Whisk all the dressing ingredients together, loosening with a little water, if necessary.

Add the salad ingredients, except the peanuts and cilantro, to the noodles. Pour over the dressing and use tongs to mix well. Transfer to a serving bowl and sprinkle with the peanuts and cilantro. Squeeze over extra lime juice.

TIP

No soybeans? Double up on the peas. Chopped green beans, snow peas, or sugar snaps all work well.

TOPPINGS

Kimchi Slaw (page 160) / Lime and Cilantro Gremolata (page 182) / Peanut Rayu (page 180)

LEFTOVER CHICKEN AND RICE SALAD

Prep: 5 min

SERVES: 1

½ cucumber

1 scallion, thinly sliced

1 red chile, thinly sliced

⅔ cup (20 g) cilantro with
stalks, finely sliced

1 tablespoon mint leaves,
finely sliced

½ cup (50 g) cooked rice
or any other grain

⅓ cup (50 g) shredded
leftover cooked chicken

DRESSING:

3 tablespoons tamari sauce

1 tablespoon rice wine
vinegar or apple
cider vinegar

½ tablespoon mirin

1 teaspoon sesame oil

1 teaspoon maple syrup

A tiny piece of
garlic, grated

This salad is good for frustration … pounding the cucumber works wonders for it.

Halve the cucumber and use a spoon to remove the seeds. Place the seeds in a food processor and blitz with the rest of the dressing ingredients.

Roughly chop the cucumber into 1¼-inch (3 cm) pieces. Place in a deep bowl along with the scallion. Using the end of a rolling pin, gently pound the cucumber and scallion together. You want to crack the skins of the cucumber. Add the remaining ingredients, except for the rice and chicken, and pour over the dressing. Let stand for 2 minutes.

Add the rice to a clean bowl and stir through the chicken. Pour the cucumber dressing over the top and enjoy.

TIPS
No chicken? Flaked smoked fish works well. White or brown rice is good, but try other grains to mix it up.

TOPPINGS
Peanut Rayu (page 180) / Mustard Seed Shallots (page 185)

TAHINI AVOCADO SALAD

Prep: 5 min
Cook: 5 min

SERVES: 1

1 tablespoon extra-virgin
   olive oil
1 slice of sourdough or
   other bread, cut into
   small cubes
1 tablespoon sesame seeds
½ cup (30 g)
   grated Parmesan
1½ cups (30 g) arugula
1 avocado, halved, peeled,
   and pitted

DRESSING:

1 tablespoon tahini
1 tablespoon olive oil
½ tablespoon lemon juice
½ teaspoon Dijon mustard
½ teaspoon honey
Salt and black pepper

To make this salad more substantial add some fish or cooked chicken at the end.

Heat the oil in a pan and drop in the bread cubes. Fry until they start to turn golden and crispy. Add the sesame seeds and Parmesan and fry until the Parmesan has melted and the seeds are golden. Tip onto paper towels and set aside.

Add the arugula to a salad bowl, then scoop the avocado out of its skin over the bowl. Whisk all the dressing ingredients together in another bowl and add 1 tablespoon of really cold water. Season and whisk until it's creamy. Drizzle generously over the salad before topping with the croutons.

TIP
No avocado? Try cooked broccoli, green beans, cauliflower, or even leftover roasted vegetables.

TOPPINGS
Kimchi Slaw (page 160) / Last of the Veg Curtido (page 164) / Yellow Zucchini Kraut (page 163) / Everyday Kraut (page 165) / All the Pinks (page 163) / Quick Onion Relish (page 179) / Nutty Pangrattato (page 174) / Creamy Green Kefir Dressing (page 179)

PANTRY RECIPES TO RELY ON

Here you will find my favorite jars brimming with goodness, so come with me and take a dive into creating flavor bombs, textural toppings, sauces to envy, and ferments to whiz, pop, and bang!

Here are five top simple ferments to feed your gut and bring life to that everyday working lunch.

KIMCHI SLAW

Prep: 35 min
Ferment: 3
days + 1 week

MAKES: 2 x 17-ounce (500 ml) jars

1 medium Chinese cabbage (2 pounds/ 900 g), cut into quarters lengthwise and cored

½ pound (225 g) daikon radish, peeled and cut into matchsticks

4 scallions, cut into ¾-inch (2 cm) pieces

1 tablespoon grated garlic (5 to 6 small cloves or 3 large)

1 teaspoon grated fresh ginger

1 teaspoon granulated sugar

2 tablespoons fish sauce

3½ tablespoons gochugaru

Sea salt

This kimchi is a quicker ferment as the cabbage is shredded as opposed to cut in chunks. Play around with the levels of garlic and ginger to suit your taste.

Shred the cabbage and place in a bowl. Add the radish and scallions, then weigh. Kimchi salt rule is 3% (e.g. 2¼ pounds / 1 kg x 0.03 = 1 ounce / 30 g). Add the correct amount of salt and massage. Leave for 30 minutes.

Rinse the cabbage, radish, and scallions and drain. Combine all the remaining ingredients in a bowl. Add the vegetables and mix, then pack into a sterilized jar (page 167) and press down. Leave a 1-inch (2.5 cm) headspace. Add a weight and seal the jar. Leave in a cool, dry place for three days, opening the lid every day (page 167). Chill for a week before using. Store in the refrigerator for up to three months.

TIP

This delicious slaw gives any lunch a certain zing. Stir through rice, add to a cheese or egg lunch, perk up any warm soup, dal, or stew. Delicious as an added crunch to warm salads, mixed in a fritter, or even a pancake.

ALL THE PINKS

Prep: 40 min
Ferment: 5 to
7 days

MAKES: 1 pound (450 g)
1 medium red cabbage
(save a few outer
layers), cored and
thinly shredded
2 beets, grated
1 carrot, grated
½ red onion, finely sliced
1 tablespoon
juniper berries
Sea salt

**Bright and cheerful in winter, this kraut brings
lunches to life.**

Place all the vegetables in a large bowl and weigh. To add
salt, follow the 2% rule on page 167. Massage the salt into
the vegetables and leave for 30 minutes. Massage again.
The cabbage should be limp and liquid should be forming
in the bowl. Pack the vegetables into a sterilized jar (page
167) with the liquid. Use a folded cabbage leaf to form a
lid and a weight to keep the vegetables submerged. Close
the lid. Keep in a cool, dark place for five to seven days,
opening the lid every day (page 167). Taste test. Store in
the refrigerator for up to six months.

YELLOW ZUCCHINI KRAUT

Prep: 10 min
Ferment:
5 days

MAKES: 1 pound (450 g)
5 small to medium
zucchini (about
1 pound / 450 g)
1 small red onion,
finely sliced
2 garlic cloves, grated
1 lemon, thinly sliced
1 teaspoon hot pepper
flakes (or less if shy)
1 teaspoon
ground turmeric
Sea salt

**Super simple with a vibrant color, this is a great recipe
when there is a glut of zucchini in the summer.**

Grate the zucchini into a large bowl. Add the remaining
ingredients, except the turmeric and salt. To add salt,
follow the 2% rule on page 167. Massage the salt through,
squeezing the juice from the vegetables. When liquid
starts to appear, add the turmeric and stir in with a spoon
to avoid staining. Spoon into a sterilized jar (page 167).
Use a folded cabbage leaf to form a lid and a weight to
keep the vegetables submerged. Close the lid. Keep in a
cool, dark place for five days, opening the lid every day
(page 167). Taste test. Store in the refrigerator for up to
three months.

LAST OF THE VEG CURTIDO

Prep: 15 min
Ferment: 10
to 14 days

MAKES: 2¼ pounds
(1 kg)

2¼ pounds (1 kg) white or
green (or a mix)
cabbage (keep one or
two of the outer
leaves), cored
and thinly shredded

2 carrots, grated

1 red onion, thinly sliced

1 tablespoon
dried oregano

2 tablespoons
sliced jalapeños

Sea salt

**A South American staple, which is delicious in a taco,
sandwich, or wrap. Try it with cheese, egg, a Buddha
bowl, soup, or simply on the side.**

Place the cabbage in a large bowl with the remaining
ingredients and weigh. To add salt, follow the 2% rule on
page 167.

Massage the vegetables until limp and liquid is forming
at the bottom of the bowl. Pack the vegetables into a
sterilized jar (page 167) with the liquid, using your
fist to push it down to remove air bubbles and release
more brine.

Use a folded cabbage leaf to form a lid and a weight to
keep the vegetables submerged. Close the lid. Keep in
a cool, dark place, opening the lid to get rid of the gas
every day (page 167). It is ready within ten to fourteen
days. Taste test. Store in the refrigerator for up to
six months.

TIP
It is a great alternative to slaw and delicious stirred
through rice. It's handy when you have some vegetables
that need using. Try carrot, radish, beet, celery root,
and scallions.

PANTRY RECIPES TO RELY ON

EVERYDAY KRAUT

Prep: 40 min
Ferment:
14 days

MAKES: 1 pound (450 g)
1 large white cabbage
   (keep one or two of the
   outer leaves), cored and
   thinly shredded
½ cucumber, sliced
1 tablespoon fennel seeds
6 black peppercorns
Sea salt

**If you are new to fermenting, try this simple "kraut."
It's very easy to follow with tasty results.**

Place all the ingredients in a large bowl and weigh. To
add salt, follow the 2% rule on page 167. Massage the salt
into the vegetables. Set aside for 30 minutes.

Massage again. The cabbage should be limp and liquid
should be forming in the bowl. Pack the vegetables into
a sterilized jar (page 167) with the liquid, using your
fist to push it down to remove the air bubbles. Use a
folded cabbage leaf to form a lid and a weight to keep the
vegetables submerged. Close the lid. Keep in a cool, dark
place for ten to fourteen days, opening the lid to get rid
of the gas every day (page 167). Taste test. Store in the
refrigerator for up to six months.

TIP
The cucumber is added for freshness, but you can omit
it for more of a pure cabbage ferment. Experiment with
flavors and spices, such as dill / caraway, lemon / ginger,
ginger / carrot, ginger / beet.

01. Sterilize the jar.

02. Remove outer leaves and rinse.

Quarter and remove core.

03. Shred and salt.

04. Pack into the jar.

05. Weigh cabbage down.

2 WEEKS

06. Place in cool, dark place.

THE WEALTH AND HEALTH OF FERMENTING

The trick to fermenting is to start simple. It can seem daunting to create ferments with a variety of vegetables and what if it goes wrong? Don't despair ... start with one, nurture it, and build up to more. This is a great way to incorporate ferments into your lunches.

WHAT DO I NEED TO MAKE KRAUT?

MAKES: 17-ounce (500 ml) jar
1 red or green cabbage
Salt, preferably noniodized, such as sea salt or kosher

What lunch can kraut be eaten with?

Toasted cheese sandwiches → soups → salads → rice → smoked fish → pancakes

Other recipes to try:

Kimchi Slaw → p160
Last of the Veg Curtido → p164
All the Pinks → p163
Everyday Kraut → p165

1. Sterilize jar → Pour boiling water over it or run it through a dishwasher.

2. Prepare cabbage → Remove outer leaves and rinse under cold running water to remove dirt. Quarter it and remove the core.

3. Shred and salt cabbage → Thinly slice or shred the cabbage using a knife. Place in a large bowl with salt. The ratio is 2% salt by weight of cabbage. For example, for 1¾ pounds (800 g) of cabbage, use ½ ounce (15 g) of salt.

4. Pack cabbage → Transfer the salted cabbage to the prepared jar and press down firmly as you pack it in to release all the liquid and remove any air bubbles.

5. Add weight → Place a weight on top of the cabbage to keep it submerged under the liquid. (Use a clean stone, a glass ferment weight, or a smaller jar filled with water.)

6. Let ferment → Place the jar in a cool, dark place for up to two weeks, checking it every two days by tasting if it is tangy and sour and to your liking. Once it's done, store it in the refrigerator. Kraut usually takes ten to fourteen days to ferment.

FERMENTING WELL

Consuming fermented foods offers various health benefits due to the presence of beneficial bacteria, enzymes, and nutrients. Here are some of the advantages of adding a ferment to your lunch.

Ferments add crunch and flavor to your lunches that you can't get anywhere else.

Probiotic → Rich in probiotics, which are beneficial bacteria that promote a healthy gut microbiome. A balanced gut microbiome is linked to improved digestion, immune function, and mental health.

Nutrient boost → The fermentation process can enhance the bioavailability of certain nutrients in foods. For example, fermented cabbage in sauerkraut can make it easier for the body to digest and absorb nutrients such as vitamins C and K.

Digestive health → Probiotics and enzymes in fermented foods can aid digestion, reduce bloating, and alleviate symptoms of irritable bowel syndrome (IBS) and other digestive issues.

Immune support → A healthy gut microbiome is closely linked to a strong immune system. Consuming ferments regularly can potentially help in strengthening your body's natural defenses against infections and illnesses.

Mental health → Some studies suggest a connection between gut health and mental wellbeing. Probiotics and other compounds in fermented foods might play a role in improving mood and reducing symptoms of anxiety.

Anti-inflammatory effects → Ferments often contain compounds with anti-inflammatory properties, which can help in reducing inflammation in the body and lowering the risk of chronic diseases.

It's important to note that while ferments can offer various health benefits, they should be consumed as part of a balanced diet and not as a sole source of probiotics or nutrients. Individuals with certain health conditions or those taking medications should consult with a healthcare professional before making significant changes to their diet, including increasing the intake of fermented foods.

A nutty crunch adds another dimension
to lunch. It smacks you with protein,
and makes food very moreish to eat.

TURMERIC ROASTED MIX

Prep: 8 min
Cook: 10 min

MAKES: 3 cups (450 g)
¼ cup (40 g) walnuts,
    coarsely chopped
Generous ⅓ cup
    (45 g) pecans,
    coarsely chopped
½ cup (60 g)
    pumpkin seeds
½ cup (70 g) sesame seeds
2 teaspoons olive oil
1 tablespoon togarashi
Zest of 1 orange
1 tablespoon
    ground turmeric
2 tablespoons black
    sesame seeds
1 tablespoon ground
    black pepper
½ teaspoon sea salt

**This crunchy mix with a little sweetness from the
orange will pimp up any dish.**

Preheat the oven to 350°F (180°C).

Toss all the ingredients together in a large bowl. Lay
out on a baking sheet and bake for 6 minutes. Stir, then
bake for another 4 minutes. Let cool before storing in a
sterilized jar (page 167) for up to 1 month.

TIP
There are countless sprinkling possibilities on all kinds
of savory dishes, from salads to soups, beans, stews, dips,
and on eggs.

SPICY PUMPKIN MIX

Prep: 2 min
Cook: 5 min

MAKES: 1½ cups (200 g)

1½ cups (200 g)
    pumpkin seeds,
    washed and dried
2 teaspoons extra-virgin
    olive oil
2 teaspoons sweet
    smoked paprika
2 teaspoons ground cumin
½ teaspoon hot
    chili powder
1 teaspoon sea salt

Handy for a simple midmorning snack, this salad and soup topper is great on a savory pancake. Add more spice if that's your vibe.

Dry-fry all the seeds in a skillet for 4 to 5 minutes until they start popping. Remove from the heat and add the remaining ingredients. Stir to combine, then let cool. Store in a clean jar for up to one month.

ZA'ATAR CHICKPEA CRUNCH

Prep: 5 min
Cook: 17 min

MAKES: 1¼ cups (200 g)

2 cups (250 g) canned
    chickpeas, drained
    and dried
1 tablespoon za'atar
1 tablespoon olive oil, plus
    extra for drizzling
2⅓ cups (100 g)
    panko breadcrumbs
Zest of 1 lemon
Sea salt

A real savory protein topper for salads, soups, stews, dals, and pastas. I've used za'atar for its savory cumin fix, but experiment with other flavors like Berbere, Chinese 5 spice, or even ras el hanout.

Preheat the oven to 480°F (250°C). Line a baking sheet with baking parchment. Blitz the chickpeas in a food processor to crumbs. Stir through the za'atar and drizzle with oil. Spread the crumbs out on the baking sheet and roast for 15 minutes. Add the oil, breadcrumbs, lemon zest, and chickpeas to a skillet. Season. Fry for 3 minutes, or until crispy. Store in a clean jar for up to one month.

NUTTY PANGRATTATO

Prep: 5 min
Cook: 5 min

MAKES: 10-ounce
(300 ml) jar
1 cup (150 g) nuts, such as
cashews, almonds,
peanuts, walnuts,
pecans, hazelnuts
1 tablespoon rosemary,
thyme, oregano, or mix
3½ cups (150 g)
panko breadcrumbs
1 tablespoon olive oil
1 teaspoon sea salt

Flexible by nature, this delicious nutty breadcrumb topping can be created with whatever nut or herb you have in your pantry.

Using a mortar and pestle, or a quick blitz in a food processor, blitz the nuts and herbs until they form crumbs. Transfer to a large bowl with the breadcrumbs and stir through the oil and salt. Transfer to a large skillet and fry over medium heat for 4 to 5 minutes until golden and crispy. Store in a clean jar for up to one month.

TIP
To boost its crispness, reheat in a hot pan for a few seconds. If you're avoiding gluten, then just omit the breadcrumbs.

These are great to create in bulk. Times the ingredients by three and you will have enough for the week.

FRENCH OOMPH DRESSING

Prep: 5 min

MAKES: Scant ½ cup
    (100 ml)
6 tablespoons extra-virgin
    olive oil
2 tablespoons white
    wine vinegar
2 teaspoons Dijon mustard
2 teaspoons honey
Salt

A "go-to" dressing for drizzling over hot potatoes, a warm chicken, and any slaw instead of mayo. Dijon is a vital ingredient here ... it pings it up a notch and has your nose tingling with joy! Use liberally.

Whisk all the ingredients together in a small bowl until it looks creamy. Add a pinch of salt, whisk and taste again. Or, add all the ingredients to a jam jar, seal and shake.

APPLE CIDER DRESSING

Prep: 6 min

MAKES: 3 ounces (90 ml)
6 tablespoons extra-
    virgin olive oil
    (not too peppery)
2 tablespoons apple
    cider vinegar
2 garlic cloves, grated
2 teaspoons floral honey
1 teaspoon hot
    pepper flakes
Sea salt

Do you love a crispy salad? This is the dressing for it. Apple cider makes a fab everyday dressing.

Place all the ingredients in a bowl or jar, and whisk or shake. Taste and season. Whisk or shake and taste again. Keep doing this until you get to the taste you like. Store in the refrigerator until you need it. You may need to bring it back to room temperature and give it a shake before reusing.

QUICK ONION RELISH

Prep: 11 min

MAKES: 3½ cups (300 g)
3½ cups (300 g)
  minced red onions
5 tablespoons rice
  wine vinegar
2 tablespoons honey
1 tablespoon thyme leaves
Sea salt

This is a regular relish I have in my refrigerator to brighten and freshen up any kind of leftovers. It also works well with egg, cheese, salads, noodles, and grain bowls. Actually I can't think of anything that doesn't go well with it.

Spoon the diced onion into a jam jar and add the vinegar, honey, and thyme. Season, seal with the lid, and shake. This pickle will get stronger the longer you leave it. Store in the refrigerator for up to one week.

CREAMY GREEN KEFIR DRESSING

Prep: 5 min

MAKES: ⅔ cup (160 ml)
Scant 1 cup (200 ml)
  plain kefir
½ cup (75 g)
  chopped avocado
1 bunch of chives
1 cup (30 g) parsley leaves
1 small garlic clove, peeled
1 tablespoon lemon juice
½ teaspoon salt
¼ teaspoon ground
  black pepper
4 anchovy fillets
3 tablespoons extra-virgin
  olive oil

This tangy dressing perks up any grilled or broiled vegetable, whether it's left over or not. It's a great way to look after the gut with the tasty addition of soft herbs and avocado.

Blitz all the ingredients together in a blender, scraping down the sides a little, making sure everything is smooth. Store in a clean jar in the refrigerator for up to three days.

A trio of mega natural flavor enhancers, these special condiments can enliven any lunchtime.

PEANUT RAYU

Prep: 10 min
Cook: 10 min

MAKES: 2⅔ cups
  (650 ml)
1¾ cups (250 g) natural
  peanuts, skinless and
  coarsely chopped
5 garlic cloves,
  thinly sliced
1 cup (240 ml)
  vegetable oil
4½ ounces (125 g)
  gochugaru or 2 ounces
  (60 g) smoked paprika
  and 2 ounces (60 g)
  sliced dried chile
½ cup (65 g)
  sesame seeds
¼ cup (60 ml)
  tamari sauce
3 tablespoons maple syrup
Scant ½ cup (100 ml)
  toasted sesame oil
1 cup (240 ml) light
  olive oil

A slight warning goes with this pantry staple—it's addictive. You may find yourself putting it on everything! That's fine, as you've made it and you also know what's in it. Enjoy!

Dry-fry the peanuts in a skillet until warmed through and slightly toasted, about 5 minutes.

Place the garlic cloves in the cold vegetable oil in a skillet. Turn the heat to medium to high and fry for 4 to 5 minutes until the garlic cloves are lightly golden and crispy. Keep an eye on them, as they can turn quickly. Using a slotted spoon, remove the garlic and let dry on paper towels.

Add the peanuts and gochugaru to the skillet off the heat. Stir and let sizzle. Once cooled, add the remaining ingredients and pour into a large jam jar. Shake. Store in the refrigerator for up to three months.

LIME AND CILANTRO GREMOLATA

Prep: 6 min
Cook: 5 min

MAKES: 1 small bowl

3 tablespoons olive oil,
  plus extra for frying
1 slice of sourdough or
  other bread, grated
  into breadcrumbs
Zest of ½ lime, plus 2
  tablespoons fresh juice
1 garlic clove,
  finely chopped
¾-inch (2 cm) piece of
  fresh ginger, peeled
  and grated
3 tablespoons chopped
  cilantro leaves
  and stalks
3 tablespoons
  fresh breadcrumbs
2 tablespoons
  sesame seeds
Salt and black pepper

This Italian flavor bomb traditionally uses parsley, garlic, and lemon. Try this version to enhance your pasta and noodle bowls, salads and potatoes.

Add a little olive oil to a skillet and fry the breadcrumbs until crispy. Drain on paper towels. When cooled, add all the ingredients to a bowl and season. Store in the refrigerator for up to three days.

TIP
For a gluten-free option, omit all the breadcrumbs and replace with a nut.

MUSTARD SEED SHALLOTS

Prep: 5 min
Cook: 20 min

MAKES: 1 jam jar
Scant ½ cup (100 ml)
    vegetable oil
2⅓ cups (400 g) banana
    shallots, sliced
2 tablespoons brown
    mustard seeds
Salt and black pepper

Heat the oil in a deep skillet or wok until it reaches 350°F (180°C), then deep-fry the shallots in batches for 3 to 4 minutes until light brown and crispy. Using a small flat strainer or slotted spoon, remove the onions and drain on paper towels. Repeat until all the onions are cooked.

Using 1 tablespoon of the cooking oil, fry the mustard seeds in another skillet until they start popping. Once popping, add to the onions and season. Store in an airtight container for three to five days.

SICILIAN MUFFULETTA

Prep: 15 min

MAKES: 1 jam jar
1 celery stalk, diced
2 garlic cloves, diced
2 red chiles, seeded
    and diced
½ teaspoon dried oregano
2 tablespoons olive oil
1 tablespoon white
    wine vinegar
4 cauliflower florets,
    finely chopped
1 carrot, peeled and
    finely chopped
⅓ cup (40 g) pimento-
    stuffed green
    olives, drained
Sea salt and black pepper

This recipe is based on a type of relish you find in Sicily. I've tweaked it and it's a fine addition to any cold leftovers, on a cracker, or even brilliant as a sandwich spread.

Stir all the ingredients together in a bowl and season to taste. Pour into a clean jar, seal with a lid, and shake. Store in the refrigerator for up to two weeks.

TIP
Blitz the ingredients in a food processor if you don't fancy a bit of therapeutic chopping.

INDEX

Hardie Grant North America
2912 Telegraph Ave
Berkeley, CA 94705
hardiegrant.com

Published in the United States by Hardie
Grant North America, an imprint of
Hardie Grant Publishing Pty Ltd.
Library of Congress Cataloging-in-
Publication Data is available upon request
ISBN: 9781958417782
ISBN: (eBook) 9781958417799

Acquisitions Editor: Catie Ziller
Photographer: Kirstie Young
Food Styling: Zoe Morris and
  Elspeth Allison
Initial Design Concept: Michelle Tilly
Designer: Alice Chadwick
Copy Editor: Kathy Steer

Printed in China

FIRST EDITION

Hardie Grant
PUBLISHING

ACKNOWLEDGMENTS

A big shout out to all the amazing
women who worked on this little
book of lunch joy! Catie Ziller,
thank you for going with this idea.
Zoe Morris and Elspeth Allison,
thank you for your brilliant food
styling support, this book would
not look like this if it wasn't for you.
Jaine Bevan, your prop cupboard
was immensely helpful, thank
you. Sophie @starlingpots, thank
you for your handy work on your
beautiful ceramics. Charlie @
littleearthquakepots for your original
pottery pieces. Michele Tilly, Alice
Chadwick, and Kathy Steer, thanks
for all your tremendous tenacity.
Kirstie Young, thank you for bringing
this book to life with your beautiful
photos. Finally, thank you to Amanda
Honey for your exceptional barn
and studio at Caisson Gardens, Bath
UK; we were so lucky to be able to
photograph at your place. And lastly
but by no means least…for Clover
and Jono, I love you!